Charley Boorman is a much-loved TV star, adventurer and number one bestselling author. His travels with Ewan McGregor were chronicled in the international bestsellers *Long Way Round* and *Long Way Down*. He is also the author of *Race to Dakar*, *By Any Means* and *Right to the Edge*.

When he is not travelling the world, he lives in London with his wife, two daughters and growing collection of motorbikes.

Also by Charley Boorman

Long Way Round (with Ewan McGregor)

Long Way Down (with Ewan McGregor)

Race to Dakar

*By Any Means: The Brand New Adventure
From Wicklow to Wollongong*

Right to the Edge: Sydney to Tokyo By Any Means

Extreme Frontiers

Racing Across Canada from Newfoundland to the Rockies

CHARLEY BOORMAN

with JEFF GULVIN

SPHERE

First published in Great Britain in 2012 by Sphere
This paperback edition published in 2013 by Sphere

A CIP catalogue record for this book
is available from the British Library.

ISBN 978-0-7515-4895-2

All photographs courtesy of Russ Malkin, Emily Malkin and Nathaniel Jessel

Map drawn by John Gilkes

Typeset in Times by M Rules
Printed and bound in Great Britain by
Clays Ltd, St Ives plc

Papers used by Sphere are from well-managed forests
and other responsible sources.

MIX
Paper from
responsible sources
FSC® C104740

Sphere
An imprint of
Little, Brown Book Group
100 Victoria Embankment
EC4Y 0DY

An Hachette UK Company
www.hachette.co.uk

www.littlebrown.co.uk

To my ever-patient wife, Olivia, and my two gorgeous daughters, Doone and Kinvara.

Also to my gorgeous mummy, Crystal, and my lovely sisters Katrina and Daisy.

Contents

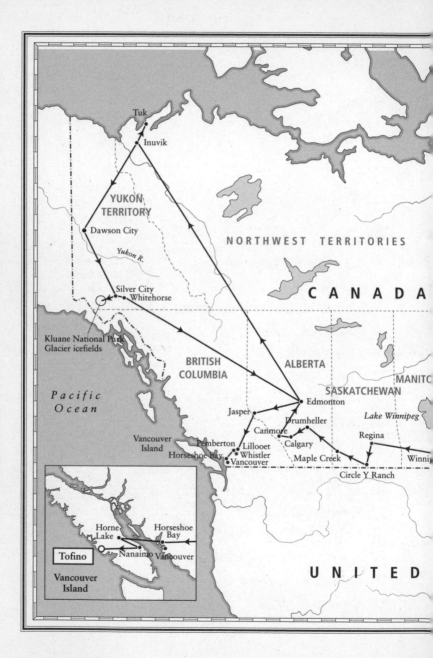

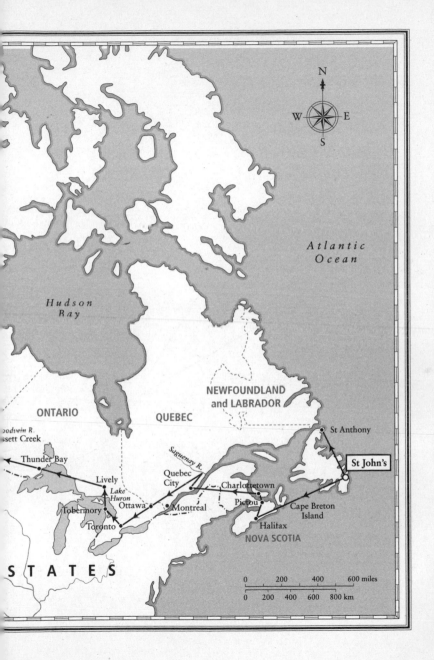

1

On the Hunt for Icebergs

Cape Spear, Newfoundland. The easternmost point of the vast land mass that is North America. It was a dank and foggy summer's day and beneath me the waves of the Atlantic crashed against the rocks; ahead of me lay a country that spreads all the way to the Pacific. Canada.

This coastline is beautiful but dangerous: savage cliffs and submerged reefs where death comes swift and terrible. Many a ship has foundered on the beachhead that jutted out just below me, and there's been a lighthouse at Cape Spear since 1836 to guide them to safety. There are now two on the headland – a classic white tower with a light at the top and the more modern one, a squat building with two holes in the walls, a light beaming horizontally from one and the horn sounding from the other.

Climbing some wooden steps from my lonely vantage point, I came to a World War II gun battery built to defend the entrance to St John's Harbour. Only the barrel of one of the guns is there now, but it's a bloody great thing – we're talking thirty feet of iron that's almost pink with age and corrosion. As I walked the length of it, I could only imagine the noise it would have made when it was fired.

Behind the battery, tunnels extend into the rock where bunkers were dug for the troops that manned this place during the war. U-boats patrolled these waters regularly, according to John, the local guide showing me around. Their mission was to destroy the supply convoys heading across the Atlantic. They were hardly ever seen and the guns were rarely if ever fired, but there was one famous occasion when a U-boat skipper ran his vessel across a submerged rock the locals call 'Old Harry'. The rudder was badly damaged and the skipper was ready to abandon ship, but his engineer figured he could fix it, so they took a chance and surfaced while he carried out the repairs.

Amazingly, this enemy submarine that should've been a sitting duck for the gunners manning the battery managed to escape completely unscathed: the engineer mended the rudder and the sub steamed away. When the locals finally discovered that a U-boat had been above the surface close to the shore, nobody could understand why it hadn't been fired on. I imagine the Germans were pretty puzzled too – the skipper must have thanked his lucky stars that after three hours in full view he was able to sail away without so much as a shot across the bows. The official word was that the gunners hadn't spotted it because it was December and there were snow squalls swirling (it's true a U-boat had a particularly low profile), but John's theory is that nobody really believed they'd *ever* see a U-boat – so when one did finally surface, they weren't paying attention.

New-found-land. Just the name is incredibly evocative, hinting at courageous explorers and perilous ocean voyages. It was way back in the eleventh century that a Viking known as Leif Erikson became the first European to set eyes on this treacherous coastline (the only confirmed Norse settlement in North America); he was followed over the years by explorers from England, France and Portugal. It is a place with a rich history, as I was already beginning to discover just moments into my expedition. What a start to this new journey, I thought: ahead of me lay seven weeks, criss-crossing this enormous and unfamiliar place with who knows what in store.

For a while now I've been reading articles in newspapers or listening to people on the TV referring to me as an 'actor and travel writer', but it's only recently that I've really begun to think about what that means. The fact is I've not done a great deal of acting lately, so I suppose that makes me primarily a travel writer. But the thing is, although I know my books are about journeys and adventures, in all honesty I'm not sure I've really got to know the places I've visited as much as I would've liked.

This was on my mind when I met up with my old friend Russ Malkin back in the spring of last year. He was aware of what was bugging me and he had this idea about pushing the boundaries of various countries in a way we never had before. He wanted to start with Canada, the second biggest country in the world and one I'd travelled to in *Long Way Round* and had always wanted to explore in more depth one day. This trip would be different: yes, it was an expedition – we'd be crossing a continent and it would be on bikes and boats and buses – but this was one, single vast country and we'd have enough time to get to know not only the place but the people properly as well.

Looking back on the trips I'd done with Ewan McGregor, we travelled huge distances and learned so much about the countries we passed through but because we were always racing against the clock, we sometimes missed opportunities to really get to know particular places and people. So while Ewan and I both have incredible memories of those trips, there's still so much of the world out there for me to discover. We'd pushed the boundaries for sure – we'd found ourselves crossing some pretty extreme frontiers – but this time the plan was to really get under the skin of the place.

So now it was 9 June, and Russ and I were starting our adventure at Canada's most easterly point, with Nat Jessel and Mungo shooting film. Newfoundland is an island of course, a land mass of 108,000 square kilometres that's separated from the Labrador Peninsula by the Strait of Belle Isle. If you grab a map and take a quick scout, you'll see that it looks a bit like the head of a deer. See what I mean? The nose points to the south-west, with the antlers rising to where the town of St Anthony, our next stop, sits way up on the northern peninsula.

We were all incredibly excited. Hunched up in cattle class on the plane over, all we could talk about was icebergs, the Arctic and the Great Lakes. This was another beginning, a new expedition – we'd go as far north as the Arctic Ocean, and we'd bump along the border with the United States to the south.

My first sight of St Anthony was the bay. It was a grizzled old bear of a summer's day, with the rock as grey and chipped as the sea beyond it. It was a funny feeling being there with the foghorn sounding its warning to ships out in the Atlantic – like a siren it seemed to mark the dawn of our journey. We stopped at an old clapboard fisherman's hut and inside we found Dean and Dave, a couple of guys we'd heard about who had been fishing the waters around this island for twenty-six seasons. They caught crab and mackerel, herring and squid, as well as seals when they could get them. This was rugged country, and Dean said that whatever there was to be had here, the people of Newfoundland made sure they got it.

'Charley,' he said, 'in this part of the world you have to do whatever you can in order to survive.'

'It's tough up here then, is it?'

At that he broke into a smile and spoke in that strangely lilting accent that seems somewhere between American and Irish.

'Tough?' he said. 'I reckon. You've got to be just to stay up here, you know.'

I've eaten crab, herring and mackerel – and calamari, of course – but I'd never tasted seal. Dean explained that there's a market for both seal meat and the pelt, but right now it wasn't quite what it had been as in recent years demand had fallen. Historically the area had been rich in cod, and in the old days Dean and Dave would catch as much as five hundred pounds each summer. But in 1992 the authorities allowed trawlers from the Grand Banks to come in, and they cleaned up all the spawning fish. As a consequence, local fishing operations like Dean and Dave's had to look to other markets.

I asked Dave how they survived in the winter; just from the landscape alone, it seemed that making a living in Newfoundland was indeed as tough as they were saying. Dave was phlegmatic. 'In the winter we go duck hunting,' he said, 'and every year we take a moose or two; pretty much every family up here needs moose if they want to make it through the winter.'

The hunting was licensed, of course, and Dean reckoned that one moose would be enough to feed his family and Dave's for most of the year.

'You've got to take care of the land, though,' he reminded me. 'You can't just go up there and shoot what you want. We try to take a young bull; the meat's good and lean because they're selective in their browsing. You need to leave the cows and calves be.'

Dave said that a lot of people who hunted moose shot them when they were grazing close to the highway. To him that wasn't hunting; he and Dean had a cabin in the woods and they'd trail their quarry on foot, follow a spoor and hunt the animal properly. It gave the moose a chance rather than just pulling up by the side of the road and blasting it. They lived off the land, picking berries, hunting meat, shooting ducks. In the summer they fished and cut the wood they'd need to heat their homes during the winter. They seemed very contented – the only thing that bothered the pair of them was that despite the fact that both of them had daughters, and Dave had grandchildren, neither of them had a son to pass their traditions on to.

'In the next eight or ten years our generation of fishing will be over,' Dean said a little wistfully. 'I mean, Dave's ready for retirement, and . . .'

At that Dave's eyebrows arched. 'I'm not dead yet,' he muttered. 'Old maybe, but not dead. Who said anything about retirement?'

While they bickered, I was staring out of the window; the mist had cleared and across the bay an iceberg climbed above the surface. It was the most beautiful thing. Suddenly I was tingling – ever since we'd first decided to come here, the one thing we'd talked about seeing was an iceberg. It occurred to me then that being men of the sea, Dean and Dave must have a boat. Maybe they'd take us over there to get a closer look. Before today I'd never even seen an iceberg, and now that I had finally clapped eyes on one, I really wanted to get up close and personal.

I decided to wait a bit, though, and get to know these boys a little better before I popped that question. In the meantime, we took a mooch around their hut. There were tools on the walls, pictures of their boat, others of Dean and Dave hunting.

On the lip of one shelf hung four number plates; one battered old white one caught my eye: 'Newfoundland and Labrador'. The easternmost of Canada's ten provinces, Newfoundland and Labrador – renamed in 2001 to recognise Labrador, a section of the mainland to the north-west that completes the province – borders Quebec, which is mostly French-speaking. I couldn't wait to see if Quebec felt like a different country altogether. Just the names of the various regions filled me with excitement: Nova Scotia, Prince Edward Island, New Brunswick, Ontario. Over the next few weeks we'd cross Manitoba and Saskatchewan, where Butch Cassidy used to hide out and Sitting Bull sought refuge after the Little Big Horn. We'd also see the Northwest Territories, Alberta, British Columbia and the Yukon.

Returning my attention to the conversation, I noticed that Dean was talking to Russ about the plots of land – the gardens or allotments – we'd seen dotted around all the way up here. He said they were individually owned; as well as catching fish and hunting, the islanders grew all their own vegetables.

'Nobody touches your garden,' he said. 'Nobody touches anything. I never lock my house and I can leave my keys in my truck without even thinking somebody might steal it.'

But about that iceberg ... 'Dean,' I said, unable to hold

back any longer, 'this might sound a little weird, but we're on the hunt for icebergs.'

'Not moose or duck, then?' Dave chipped in.

'No, icebergs. You see, we don't really get many of them where we live, and I've noticed one out there.' I pointed through the window. 'The last iceberg I saw was the one Kate Winslet smashed into. Since you guys have a boat, I was wondering . . . '

I was giving him my best doe eyes, but I wasn't sure it was working. 'Do you think you could take us out there, maybe?' I finished, hopefully.

'Oh sure,' he said. 'I don't see why not. Weather's good and we hunt icebergs all the time up here, don't we, Dave?'

I stared at him in surprise. Was he pulling my leg?

'I'm serious,' he said. 'We go out and find a piece that's broken off, bring it home and stick it in the freezer. Whenever we want ice for a drink, we just chip off a flake or two.'

Apparently he was serious. He told me that when you put the iceberg chip in the glass, the ice cracks and crackles a bit, but it doesn't taste of salt and it's great in a cocktail.

*

The three of us jumped into Dave's pickup and headed off through the outskirts of town. It was raining now; the landscape was gloomy but incredibly atmospheric.

We drove down past the St Anthony seafood plant to where their boat *Patey's Venture* was moored alongside the wooden dock. The boat was really pretty: white and green with a dinghy tied above the wheelhouse. It really was a wild old day, with rain slanting in, the clouds low and the dock slick as an ice rink. Moments later we cast off and were heading across the bay towards the iceberg.

This was a great start. I mean, things could hardly have been better! We had barely arrived in Canada and already we'd run into these two fellers who were happy to take us out in their fishing boat. In the wheelhouse, Dean told me that it was a six-hour steam out to their crab gear, and they'd leave the dock at midnight so that they would have as much daylight as possible to haul the pots. But it was dangerous. The bay was littered with sections of broken-off iceberg that floated just below the radar, and in the darkness you might not pick them up. Clattering into a chunk in the dark was not to be recommended – ice like that would sink a boat this size, and it would do it quickly. In water that cold without a survival suit you'd never last long enough to be rescued, and you would barely have time to get the suit on.

'Man, I hope you've got good insurance,' I remarked.

'Oh, we're covered pretty good, yeah. The women, they don't have to worry.' Then he pointed through the windscreen. 'There it is, right there.'

I was so excited that I was on deck in a flash, hanging on to a chain to keep from toppling overboard. I've seen glaciers when I've been skiing, and I've seen ice hanging off mountains, but encountering this enormous block of ice in the open sea was different. I was amazed to see that it was actually a very pale blue, not white at all. Running from the top of the iceberg to the bottom was a strip of deeper blue, as if someone had hopped over there and painted a stripe on it. In the wheelhouse, Russ asked Dean about it. 'It's got to be a crack, hasn't it?' he said.

'Yep, pretty much,' the skipper told him. 'Different parts of the ice are at different temperatures, and the result is that deep blue fissure you can see right there.'

Only a small portion of the berg was showing, of course: it's easy to forget that only a tiny section actually breaks the surface. Dean reckoned that this one was sitting in about twenty fathoms of water; with six feet to a fathom, that was at least one hundred and twenty feet deep. It was mind-blowing. I mean, we'd seen some sights on our travels, but this was just awesome. On an otherwise grey day it was like a sculpture, and as we came around the tip we could see that it actually broke the surface in two places, with a sweeping dip between them that formed a foaming bay of water right in the middle. The water around the base of the berg was lighter than the rest of the sea as it reflected the depth of the ice.

'Look at the colours!' Even Dean was impressed, and he lived here and saw icebergs all the time. 'What a spot to go through, right there.'

'Hey, Charley,' Russ called, laughing. 'Dean's going to drive through the gap.'

'Yeah, right,' I said, gazing at the ice just below the surface, 'and I'm going to get in the lifeboat.'

From the shore it had appeared just like any other iceberg, I suppose, but as we got close, it was like gazing on the horns of some mythical leviathan; some giant of the deep.

'All right, Dean,' Russ called. 'Take us in close, lad. We need some ice for our rum and Coke tonight.'

He was serious. Moments later we were both on deck and Russ was demanding a hammer. Eagle-eyed, he'd spotted where some of the ice had broken away, and was determined to chill his drink with North Atlantic iceberg. Sweat beading his brow, the skipper eased us in closer and closer. Russ got behind me, gripping the chain overhead, and told me to lean out; he'd make sure I didn't fall.

I don't even *like* rum and Coke, I thought to myself. I'd

prefer a nice glass of Sancerre, and you don't need ice for Sancerre. But there I was, leaning over the rail, clutching the hand axe Dave had just given me.

We edged close to where one section of the ice formed a gentle slope that might be accessible – the water below us was white now, and we could see ice perilously close to the hull. I had one foot over the side, axe in hand, with Russ holding me by the scruff of the neck. I was almost there, about to slice off a chunk, when the boat drifted away; Dean couldn't hold the position.

We weren't about to give up now, though. Straddling the rail again, I told Russ to grab a boathook as a chunk that had already broken off came floating by. I was scrabbling with the axe, Dave had another hook, and between us we tried to land the floater like we would a gaffed fish. Dumping the axe, I found another boathook, and at last we had it! Dave on one end, me on the other – I was all but over the side. Inch by inch we lifted the chunk of ice, then the hooks slipped and we lost it again to the sea.

'Have you got a net?' Russ was desperate now, and I was as determined to land the thing as he was. Dean backed the boat up and we were in business again, Dave and I with boathooks while Russ leaned over and hacked off a chunk with the axe. He lost it, couldn't grab it. 'It's going under the boat! It's going under the boat!' he was yelling at the top of his voice, and I imagined Roy Scheider in his rubbers with the great white shark diving beneath the hull.

God knows what we looked like. All you could see were two pairs of legs and the soles of our feet as we scrabbled with our prey while the fishermen looked on. Eventually Dean had had enough.

'All right,' he said. 'Get out of the way! Out of the way, you landlubbers.' He found a grey plastic fish-packing pallet, and with Dave on the hook they heaved a hunk of broken iceberg into the pallet and finally hauled it on deck.

We were soaking. Russ was clapping his hands and hopping from one foot to the other, while Dean just stood there shaking his head. 'Crazy people do crazy things,' he said. 'And you two are crazy for sure.'

On the way back, Dean and Dave told us a terrifying story. In the winter of 2007, while hunting seals, they became stuck in eighty miles of drifting pack ice along with about a hundred other boats. It was like nothing any of them had ever experienced before. Their boat was one of six that was actually lifted out of the water to rest on an ice pan. The Canadian government sent every breaker at its disposal to the area and seventy people were airlifted out by helicopter, but the crew of the *Patey* would not leave the boat. She was their livelihood and worth a couple of hundred thousand dollars; they couldn't just abandon her to chance. They showed us a diary they kept while they were out there. 'Day thirty-eight,' Russ read. 'Still stuck in the ice and morale is low. Perry is frying ham for breakfast; the coastguard is coming for us. We're still stuck in ice. We're still stuck in ice.'

He went on to read an entry Dean had written a little later. 'Still stuck. I spoke to Megan today. After I got off the phone from her she made me cry.' Megan was his daughter, and for a moment we all felt a little of his anguish. Then Russ read on. 'Perry is still shooting shit, though. He's full of it.'

Dean told us that the diary had been published in the magazine *The National Fisherman* and people all around the world had been able to read it.

'We were OK, I suppose,' he said. 'We had eight hundred gallons of fuel on board, so we had plenty of heat, and there was enough food; the only thing we didn't have plenty of was sex!'

There had been five men on the boat, one of them always on watch while the others slept in a tiny cabin right in the prow with the bunks in two tiers, one edge all but touching the bunk on the other side. I could hardly imagine it. It must've been like being in prison, only there were no bars to keep them there; just a sheet of ice.

Back on shore we said our goodbyes. Meeting Dean and Dave had been a real treat and exactly what I'd been hoping for from this trip. If all my experiences were going to be as rewarding, then it was going to be one hell of a trip.

2
Shuck and Chuck

Leaving the boat, we headed into St Anthony in search of a drink to put our 20,000-year-old ice in, some food and perhaps some Newfoundland craic as well. As we made our way downtown, we came across a good old-fashioned Irish bar called O'Reilly's. I've mentioned the accent already – there really is a lot of Irish in it, which makes this home from home for a Wicklow boy like me. Inside the bar a guy was performing some weird kind of song. Or at least I think that's what it was. Dressed in fisherman's oilskins, he was dancing around and slapping his palm with a canoe paddle, giving up a kind of staccato rap while the crowd clapped along.

After another verse or two the singer stopped and called

across the floor to a member of the audience. 'Feller,' he said, 'what's your name?'

'Greg,' replied a young guy with a pint of Guinness in front of him.

'All right, Greg. Where are you from?'

'Ottawa.'

'Ah.' The singer cocked an eyebrow. 'Down from the ivory tower then, are you?'

That must have been an in-joke, because suddenly everyone except us was laughing. Then, maybe just because we weren't laughing, the singer turned his beady eye on me. 'And what's your name, feller?'

'Charley,' I said, on my feet now and ready for whatever he was going to toss my way.

'And Charley, where are you from?'

'London.'

'Oh,' he said, putting on a mock-cockney accent now. 'We've got one from across the pond, we do.'

He was a screecher. That's what they call the sort of half-chant, half-song he'd been performing. As we sat at the bar, he explained that it was a tradition that had been going on among fishing communities for generations – I guess you could call it a sort of shanty. He told me that years ago, his father had entered a talent contest but hadn't known what to perform so had asked his own father. The old man, who had been fishing the Labrador coast all his life, had spoken of this sailing tradition. This guy had listened to his father and taken up the screech himself.

There was more to it than just the verse, though; in the bar he'd pick on a newcomer and slap them across the back of the head to see if they had the mettle to be a 'Newfie'. Part of the deal was kissing a cod. Yeah, I know, a cod – and I was the one who had to kiss it, puckering up my lips and planting a smacker right on its greasy mouth. The screecher told me that in the old days the fishermen traded fish for rum with the Jamaicans, so after the fish-kissing the newcomer had to down a shot. Soon, suitably slapped and fish-kissed and having downed the rum in one, I found myself on my knees with an oilskin hat on my head being dubbed (against my host's better judgement) an honorary Newfie.

We spent the night in St Anthony, bedding down in a B&B while rain swept the coast. I could easily imagine this landscape as Leif Erikson might have seen it, all those centuries ago. And the next morning, with the wind howling across the tussocks of grass, we made our way to the Viking settlement at L'Anse aux Meadows in the bitter cold. I couldn't quite get my head around how cold it actually was here, given the time of year. God knows what it must be like in winter. The remains of the settlement were discovered in 1960 and the site proved that Europeans had been on the North American continent long before Christopher Columbus. Since then it has been rebuilt to look exactly as it would have done when the Vikings were here; it's a snapshot of how they lived in the days of Leif Erikson.

My guide was a local historian, Agill, who was dressed like a Viking in buckskin trousers and moccasin-type boots tied with strips of rawhide. Seated by a traditional peat fire in the massive main hut, I asked him what it would've been like back in the eleventh century. There's one large building in the reconstructed settlement, together with a couple of smaller ones. Each hut was made exactly as it would have been a thousand years ago, with a post-and-reed framework and peat-brick walls. The walls are two metres thick to keep out the cold. It would have been warm and dry, if a little smoky from the fires they kept burning. Agill reckoned these buildings would have lasted for about twenty years. We were looking out on another peat-walled hut that was open on one side, with a turf roof and a kind of stone anvil sited in the entrance. Beyond that the land was desolate – and I mean to the point of being quite eerie – and he told me he thought this was the same view they would have had a thousand years previously. The hut was littered with Viking memorabilia –

21

in one corner was a wooden chest, in another a bunch of shields, swords and helmets.

This place had been a jumping-off point from where the Vikings sailed south or west or back the way they had come. Agill told us that they didn't sail by the stars; during Greenland's summer it is daylight all the time and there are no stars to guide the way. So they navigated by always keeping land in sight, island to island, iceberg to iceberg, until finally they bumped up against their destination.

It was in this village that iron was first smelted on the American continent. There is a reconstructed smithy where a ground-level double bellows contraption heats a peat fire, which smoulders until it reaches the required temperature. I watched as a blacksmith worked away at the bellows, pumping each side in turn until the fire was hot enough for the iron to be shaped. The guy told me that smelting iron was a two-man operation. If he'd been the blacksmith to the real settlement, his son would be working with him. But he didn't have a son as apprentice; he had a Charley instead.

He soon had me hunkered down, working each massive bellow individually while he piled coals on the already red-hot flames with his bare hands. Of course I got it wrong. There I was, feeling like Gandalf in a hobbit hole, when he told me I wasn't consistent with my strokes. Apparently I was pausing between them instead of maintaining a perfect one-two rhythm. It was important; a pause meant the bellows were blowing in a sort of puff-puff, if you see what I mean. What you need is a continuous stream of air with no gap, to make sure the temperature remains constant.

We were making nails – a length of iron went in the flames, and when it was hot enough, the blacksmith would retrieve it with tongs, then cut off a section and hammer it into shape on the anvil. It was with nails like this that the Vikings would fix the overlapping planks on their boats and pin the wooden frames of the buildings. It was incredible to see it being done now just as it had been a millennium before. I had a go myself and found out just how important the consistency of the heat is. I sort of managed half a nail, but I have to admit that I've got some serious time to put in before I can claim to be any kind of blacksmith.

Early the following morning we took a plane south-west to Nova Scotia, at only 53,000 square kilometres the second smallest province of Canada. Mind you, even though it's seven times smaller in land mass, the population is almost double that of Newfoundland and Labrador.

Having experienced how Vikings in Leif Erikson's day had lived and worked, we thought that some time on a raft would give us a feel for how they must've felt when they first sought a place to land. We'd managed to pick up a flight after hearing about the tidal-bore river run at a place called Maitland.

We met Burton, one of the river guides, on the road above the Shubenacadie River. He told me that the plan was to travel six miles downstream, where we'd encounter the tidal bore, the point at which the leading edge of the incoming tide meets the outgoing water. It was quite a thought, especially when Burton explained that, depending on the weather, the bore could be anything between a ripple and a wave a dozen feet high. Tidal bores aren't unique to this stretch of waterway – they occur on the River Severn, for example, back home, but that's only on the spring tide; what we were going to experience happens every twelve and a half hours.

The view from where we were standing was truly impressive; the outgoing water making a sweep around a series of massive flattened sandbars alongside a section of open water. The sandbars were the key – deep water would hit them, creating shallows that would dance with standing waves, and that was where we'd be trying to surf them.

After a quick safety briefing, we made our way down to the boats. Burton told me to be careful because the walls of the canyon were greasy with river mud. Too late. Before I knew it I was arse over tit and my oilskins were covered in gunk. Never mind, I was soon zipped into my life jacket and in one of two boats with another guide called Corey. He was going to pilot our boat while Burton navigated for Mungo, Nat and Russ. I'm sure it was so they could film my death and push up the price for the TV show.

This was more like it! OK, so it was hardly a Viking longboat, but I felt like one of the first adventurers, racing downriver with the wind in my hair. We hit the tide just before the bridge – what initially looked like a river-wide ripple coming at us actually threw the boat clean in the air – and in an instant we were riding the wave back the way we had come, like surfers. Seeing the way the incoming water raced towards you several feet higher than the water you were on . . . well, it was like smacking into a flood.

We'd had quite a watery beginning to our Canadian adventure and as we left the river I cast my mind back to the amazing iceberg we'd seen out on the boat with Dean and Dave. It was an iceberg that caused one of the worst disasters there has ever been at sea – the sinking of the *Titanic*, of course. I was thinking about that now, because we were on our way to find out more about the history of the tragedy. We were making for the provincial capital, Halifax, and to get there we'd be riding a couple of BMWs.

*

Not bad, eh? On this continent for just three-and-a-half days and already I was on two wheels. It felt just right. Coming up to the toll bridge outside Halifax, I asked the attendant if I could pay for both Russ's bike and mine, and he said, 'Of course you can, Charley.' He recognised me, told me his wife was a big fan and even wanted to take my picture. Of course I obliged him – he was the first guy since we'd landed who actually knew who I was!

Leaving one happy attendant behind us, we crossed the bridge and rode into Halifax, Nova Scotia. I loved the sound of that, I loved the way the name rolled off the tongue; like Newfoundland, it evoked all kinds of images. Right then one was uppermost in my mind: a state-of-the-art passenger liner gliding across the ocean one dark night with a mountain of ice blocking her way. Ninety-nine years later, we were on our way to Fairview Cemetery to pay our respects to some of those who died on the *Titanic*.

Fairview is a large cemetery situated just off the main highway. It is very calm and quiet and very, very sad. We were met by local guide Mark Barnett, who told us that it is the resting place of more *Titanic* victims than any other graveyard in the world, save the bottom of the ocean. He took us to the section where the victims lay, and I found myself a little choked up.

I've suffered loss in my family; my sister Telsche died of

cancer, and the fact that there's somewhere we can go to still be with her has always been so comforting. But here, thirty per cent of the small marble stones carried no name. Amazingly, the effort to identify the unknown victims still goes on – the names of two women were established only recently from original information held by the coroner. One was recovered from the water wearing a shawl with the initials L.H. stitched into it; the initials didn't correspond with any of the names on the passenger list, but years later researchers found out that she was Jenny Lovisa Henrikkson from Finland, who had always been known by her middle name.

Three hundred and twenty-nine bodies were recovered from the site of the sinking; one hundred and nineteen were buried at sea and the rest were brought to Halifax. Eighty-six of those were taken home to be buried by relatives, and the remainder were interred at Fairview. Each stone has a number signifying when the body was brought out of the water. Even among all this sadness, one really tragic story sticks out. Alma Paulson from Sweden went down with her four children, though hers was the only body recovered. Her husband Nils had come to America a year earlier to find work and set up home in Chicago, as so many immigrants did. His family were on their way to be reunited with him when the *Titanic* struck that iceberg. Alma's stone is larger than the others in the cemetery: her husband paid for it so he could include the fact that his children were lost to him too. You can only imagine how Nils Paulson must have felt when he heard the ship had gone down and his entire family had drowned. It makes you wonder what happened to him. How did he cope with such tragedy? Did he stay in Chicago? Did he go home to Sweden? I imagine his loss was compounded by the fact that most of the dead buried at Fairview were men. The 'women and children first' edict had been adhered to, and only ten female bodies were recovered. That kind of chivalry is personified in the headstone of crewman Everett Edward Elliott, aged just twenty-four. Below his name is the inscription 'Each man stood at his post while all the weaker ones went by, and showed once more to all the world how Englishmen should die.'

We went down the hill to where violin player John Law Hume is buried, one of the three band members recovered from the water, identified by their uniforms. Among fresh flowers at the stone, somebody had left a photo of him – these were the guys who famously kept on playing right to the very end.

In the movie *Titanic*, Leonardo DiCaprio's character is called Jack Dawson – a third-class passenger who won his ticket in a card game. Mark showed me a stone bearing the name J. Dawson – Joseph Dawson, actually, who'd been a coal trimmer in the ship's engine room. Who knows if the name is a coincidence or not ... we'll have to ask James Cameron.

Many maritime laws were changed after 1912 – we all know about the *Titanic*'s lifeboats and how there wasn't enough space for everyone – but just as importantly, the rules about telegraph operators changed as well. At eleven p.m. on the night of the sinking, the operator on a nearby ship, the *Californian*, signed off and went to bed. That ship was in sight of the *Titanic* just after she went down; if there had been another operator to take his place, help would have reached the stricken vessel much sooner.

The graves at Fairview are spread out in an arc that represents the side of the ship, with a gap at the front before the first headstone, which is of an unknown child whose body was never claimed. Every year since the disaster, a wreath has been laid at his stone; finally, in 2007, he was identified from a DNA sample as a boy from Wiltshire who had been travelling third class. His name was Sidney Goodwin.

The following morning we woke early. At 3.30 a.m., I was sitting at a table in the hotel in Little River where we'd stayed the night, tucking into my cornflakes and coffee. The night before, we'd bumped into a family who had fished local waters for lobster for generations. They told us we could come along with them if we wanted, only we'd have to be up early. I've never been lobster-potting before and it seemed like a good idea. At least it did until the alarm went off and I had to crawl out of my warm bed at an hour that was ungodly even by my standards. They leave the dock early to avoid the wind, because apparently it's calmer in the wee small hours. The one saving grace of the whole affair was that if we did manage to bring in some lobster, then lunch really was going to be something.

Down at the wharf, we waited in the darkness for the crew to show up. Four o'clock in the morning and the sea was indeed very calm, very beautiful in the stillness. Finally a couple of guys arrived and took us down to where their boat was tied up in its own little bay. The *Briton Cove Bounty*, built in New South Wales, Australia, was not very big, but she looked gorgeous as the sun began to drift against the horizon.

The skipper was Merril McInnes, a grey-haired guy with glasses and a baseball hat who had been fishing these waters all his life. In the season they fish six days a week and have Sundays off, so they'd missed yesterday, and instead of a couple of hundred pots to bring up, there were over four hundred. Hearing that, I felt like some crewman from *Deadliest Catch*.

I was itching to get out there, but we were waiting on Merril's two daughters, who were running very late. The bait was loaded, we were ready to cast off, but still we had to wait. Merril reckoned they had a good excuse, though: his eldest girl had just had her first child, and the baby had been crying when Merril left the house. When they finally arrived and we got the boat away from the dock, I have to say I was really quite excited. As the sun came up, we got a good look at the harbour – bordered by boulders, it cut a swathe through a purple sea.

Sitting in the wheelhouse, Merril told me about how the lobster industry had started in this area. Back in the day, when the province was only just settled, a Presbyterian minister decreed that every family should have fishing rights to a section of the water extending to two hundred acres. That equates to about twelve hundred feet of water for each family, and it was an ingenious way of making sure that each fisherman had a decent shot at making a living. It also ensured that they had to take care of their patch and not overfish it, or there would be nothing there for future generations. When Merril finally retires, his daughters will carry on, which will make five generations of the McInnes family fishing their piece of the bay.

Arriving at the first buoy, we threw the hook, catching the line and hauling it up to flip over the hydraulic block. Up came the pots, some with lobster and some without. The little ones were tossed back, but those big enough to keep were banded, their claws closed with rubber bands, before they went into the tank. While the girls and I sorted the catch, the pots were rebaited and went straight back to the bottom. And so it went on, pot after pot after pot, Boorman doing battle with lobsters determined to snip off his fingers.

The season only lasts nine weeks, but from what the girls were telling me, it makes them enough money for the entire year. The really choice lobsters – the big ones with decent-sized claws – are tagged with a code so that any restaurant or shop selling live ones can trace them back to the McInnes family.

Working with the girls was great fun – they were a really sassy pair who knew the lobster business every bit as well as their dad – but four hundred and thirteen is a lot of lobster pots, and when we were finally done, eight hours later, I was absolutely knackered. Once the last pot was back in the sea, I hosed down the deck and swept the debris over the side. I have to tell you, though, when we started steaming back and I was leaning against the rail with the wake kicking up, I didn't regret my day's hard labour. This is the kind of back-breaking work that Nova Scotia families have been doing for generations, and though I'm not sure I could do it, it is a wonderful way to keep a family together, and with so many of them involved, it gives the entire community a tremendous sense of continuity. On top of that, it only lasts a couple of months, after which they have the rest of the year to play.

Back on shore, it was time to eat some of what we'd caught, so with a little help from one of the best chefs in the Arctic, I dressed the lobster and carried them out to the hungry crew.

We hit the road once more, heading on our bikes for the ferry that would take us across the water to the smallest of Canada's ten provinces, Prince Edward Island. After a hard day's fishing, it was good to be able to doss around on a BMW for a while, weaving in and out of the traffic, sliding the back wheel in the rain and doing pirouettes standing on the seat. I'm particularly keen on side-saddle these days, one hand on the throttle, legs crossed, enjoying a good cigar. There's something about the GS1200 that just fits me – it's a touring bike that's comfortable enough for the long run and yet still so much fun.

On the crossing over it was cold, the sky leaden, the sea the colour of slate. But we were on the move and we'd had a little tarmac under the wheels and there is nothing to beat that. Our destination was Charlottetown, which was where the whole idea of Canada actually started. I was up for a bit of history; a major part of what we were trying to do here was to get under the skin of the place, and I admit I didn't really know much about it.

When we docked on Prince Edward Island, the heavy trucks rolled off first – the massive Macks and Kenworths, the kind of thing I'd driven in Australia on *By Any Means*. I had to pop a wheelie, of course; I mean, this was a new province and the bikes had to be christened properly, and that meant on the back wheel. The road was quite delicious, as my old mate Alain de Cadenet would say; a two-lane blacktop, it slithered through the countryside along a series of undulating hills with thick woodland on either side. I really wished the weather would pick up, though – this was summer, after all, and there had been no sign of the sun whatsoever.

Gradually the landscape began to open out, the trees replaced by grassland and ploughed fields, and soon we were in Charlottetown. It was really pretty, with pristine clapboard buildings and a sense of cleanliness that you don't get in many cities. We pulled up outside Government House and were met by Catherine, a wonderfully fun lady with glasses and white hair who described herself not as a local historian, but rather as a heritage activist. That sounded much funkier, and I liked her immediately. She told us that back in 1864, this was where officials from what was then referred to as

Upper and Lower Canada had gathered to discuss whether the separate provinces should join together. At that time the whole place was ruled from London and there was no such thing as 'Canada' as we know it today. Once the initial get-together was over, the various delegates met again in Quebec the following month, and in 1866 they were in London to agree all the documents. In early 1867, the whole thing was signed, sealed and delivered.

I'd got my history wrong, of course. Catherine told me that Charlottetown isn't the birthplace of Canada as I'd thought, but the birthplace of 'confederation'. That cleared up, we went inside the beautiful building. Catherine took me to a long room at the end of a lengthy corridor and there before us was the very table where the fathers of confederation had thrashed out the details of their agreement. On the wall there was a painting of men in frock coats with long sideburns and serious faces. It hadn't all been work, though; Catherine reckoned they'd had a lot of champagne to help them come to the right decision.

Strangely enough – given that the conference took place on Prince Edward Island and the rest of Canada signed up to confederation in 1867 – Prince Edward Island itself was determined not to join, and only succumbed to the pressure in 1873. Initially the people didn't see much point in a confederation – the place was humming, shipbuilding was a major industry and the trade routes were good, particularly with England.

'We set up the whole thing,' Catherine told me, 'then stood back with our arms folded for six years before we signed up.'

In another room she showed me an 1864 photograph taken on the steps of Government House, explaining that the vision had been 'Sir John A's' originally. I must have looked puzzled, because she quickly added that she was talking about Sir John A. Macdonald, the first prime minister of the new confederation. She told me plenty about the fathers of confederation, but she also told me that their wives played a really important role in trying to create an aura of congeniality. It all seemed so civilised, and Catherine explained that the islanders were still known for their friendliness towards visitors. It was true; we'd had nothing but fantastic hospitality ever since we landed.

I really liked Catherine; she was so vibrant and enthusiastic about everything. Definitely an activist. We had to say goodbye, though, and made our way downtown to Lot 30, a fine-dining restaurant owned by a guy called Gordon. I knew I must have found the right place when I spotted the Triumph Speed Triple he'd told me he rode.

Making our way inside, we cut through the kitchens and asked the chefs if Gordon was around. He came in from the front of house – a cool dude wearing jeans, biking boots and a leather waistcoat, with a bandanna tied around his head. The plan was to hook up with his mate John, another restaurateur who used to work at the oyster beds. I love shellfish, did I ever mention that? I'd already eaten lobster and today we'd be shucking oysters, so as far as I was concerned, life couldn't get much better.

We rode down to Carr's Wharfside Market, where John met us. He had long hair and was wearing a beanie hat, and his restaurant was a seafood place, of course. He showed us the oyster packing plant and explained that the shellfish were kept offshore, with the market harvesting only what they were going to ship right away.

The place was incredible; it smelled just like the ocean, with crates of oysters being soaked in a constant stream of water. According to John, it was all about the water; the best oysters are kept in the best water, and the water off Prince Edward Island is second to none. It's a labour-intensive business, mind you, running that kind of seafood market. There is little or no machinery; all the work is done by hand, because oysters have to be nurtured.

They're brought ashore in a raw state by the fishermen, and once they're at Carr's, they're sorted, dipped in lime, then returned to the water in what are called private beds. Over the next fourteen days they're regularly handled and tested to make sure they're of the highest quality. Apparently there are two types of oyster, standard and choice. The choice one is smaller and fuller in the shell, and according to John, a little easier to shuck. John introduced us to Philip, whose job it is to grade the oysters, and he told me the work is so intensive he even dreams about shellfish at night.

Hopping into a dinghy, we headed out to the private beds. (Now might be a good time to remind you that I actually hate boats; I'm not good at sea. And yet I'd done nothing but hop from one boat to another ever since I got here.) These beds, dotted all around the bay, are where they re-lay the oysters. Philip used a pair of massive tongs that looked like two garden rakes stuck together to bite into the seabed and bring up the catch he had re-laid a few days before. Now I could see just how tough a job this is. There's money to be made, of course, but only if you can sell your oysters, and that all depends on the quality. I had a go with the tongs. I could feel the shells through the mud with the prongs, but getting them up in any number was another matter altogether. I know I was born to eat oysters, I'm just not sure I was born to catch them, you know what I mean? Compared with catching lobsters even, this seemed like seriously hard graft, and after just two attempts my arms were killing me.

I asked Gordon what he thought was the best way to eat oysters, given that he was an expert.

'Naked,' he said. 'Right out of the water and shucked from the shell, with maybe a squeeze of lemon juice.'

'Naked,' I repeated, laughing. 'For a minute there I thought you meant *I* should be naked.'

'Naked with your lady maybe,' he said. 'Yeah, you could do that. Get a little bit of zing going, huh?'

'Yeah, well. You know what they say about oysters.'

He was right, of course. Straight from the shell was best, although I have been known to sprinkle the odd one with a hint of Tabasco. While we were joking, Philip brought up the mother of all oysters – way bigger than the choice ones he had re-laid. It was enormous, and when Gordon got his knife out and shucked the shell, the meat inside was big and fleshy, oily like an egg white.

'You want it, Charley?' he asked me.

'You know what?' I said. 'I think it's too big. If I ate that I'd probably hurl.'

'OK.' He looked at me, smiling. 'I reckon it must be fifteen years old, but I've got to do it.' So he sucked it down. Eyes watering, with half of it dangling down his chin, he chewed hard and finally swallowed it. 'Pretty large,' he said, grimacing. 'One of the biggest I've ever eaten.' Then he chucked the shell into the sea, as was customary. 'Jeez,' he said. 'That was a gagger for sure.'

Philip shucked me a much smaller and more delicate

oyster and it was really good, full of the taste of the sea; shucked and chucked and eaten right there on the boat. They don't come much fresher than that.

Back at the dock, it was on the bikes again, with Gordon leading the way to John's restaurant. It's called Ship to Shore and is situated on a section of coastline dotted with colonial-style homes with sweeping driveways. Gordon told me that John, a former shucking champion, was definitely the 'Mr Oyster' of the island – he knew all there was to know about crustaceans and in another life might well have even been an oyster.

Mr Oyster had gone ahead to get things ready and was inside the restaurant, all ready with a plate of oysters and a chilled bottle of wine on the counter waiting for us. The ones he was serving were five to eight years old, which made for really good eating and they were, of course, the best quality. John started shucking, and man, could he shuck. He worked his knife under the shell and a moment later the thing was opened perfectly – no grit, no slivers of shell. In his words, the oyster didn't even know that it was open. Gordon told me that in competition it's not only the speed with which the oyster can be shucked that is judged, but how well. Given that it takes between five and eight years to grow one fit for a restaurant table, it has to be perfectly presented. John could open one every four or five seconds and they all looked like the pristine example on the plate before me.

For the past fifty-two years, the world oyster shucking championships have taken place in Galway, Ireland, and John had been over three times. There is no prize money on offer, just the glory. (Although John told me that if you're known as a world-class shucker, then of course you get more trade.) Me, I'm not the best at opening the shells, but when it comes to eating them, the old Boorman magic just seems to kick in. All it takes is a chilled glass of wine and, in this case, some salt, vinegar and cracked black pepper.

3

Deliverance

By the time we hit New Brunswick, I was full of it. I had four hours' off-road biking to look forward to and I could not wait. So far we'd only been on tarmac, but I grew up riding off road in the woods and hills around my father's place at Annamoe. God, those were the days: carefree, fun-filled; if I wasn't blatting through the green lanes I was floating down the Avonmore on an inner tube.

Life goes by so fast. Now I have teenage children of my own, but it seems only yesterday that I was just a teenager myself. I know what you're thinking: you still are, Charley, you still are. And it's true in a way, I suppose. My dad's always telling me that he's spent his life swimming against the current, while I've spent mine bobbing downstream.

*

Although Quebec is the main French-spreaking Canadian province, a third of the population of New Brunswick speak it as their first language, and constitutionally the province is the only one that's listed as bilingual. New Brunswick borders Quebec and Nova Scotia and opens on to the Gulf of St Lawrence on its north-eastern boundary. We hooked up with a few of the English-speakers, a bunch of guys who run the New Brunswick Dual Sport Club. The guide was a heavy-set guy called Mike, with cropped hair and a wide smile. He mentioned that my 250cc dirt bike was brand new and that I had to break it in for him Charley Boorman style. I hadn't been on a dirt bike in a while, though, so I thought I ought to get my excuses in early ... you know, the dodgy knee and dodgy arm, the dodgy head, that kind of thing.

Mike led the way deep into the woodland to a bespoke but very narrow enduro trail. The truth is, I felt a tad rusty, but you don't really ever lose it, and once the adrenalin started to fully kick in, I was back in the groove. There was this one corner, mind you, that caught me out every time – a sharp left-hander where the trail fell away, the front wheel dug in and I was over the handlebars with memories of my crash at the Dakar Rally in 2006 flying through my head. Every time I took that bend it was the same, and after a while it really began to piss me off. What should have been a fun morning was rapidly becoming a pain in the arse.

We were riding on land belonging to the family of one of the guys in the group, Denis Landry: the woods were his, the accursed enduro course was his and the wild blueberry fields surrounding the woods belonged to him as well. I had no idea there was any difference between wild blueberries and the cultivated ones, but apparently there is – the wild berries are smaller and sweeter. The season is short, about three weeks, and these fields would not be harvested until August. They don't use pesticides or chemicals of any kind, and the berries are fertilised naturally ... as demonstrated by one of the riders, who took a pee in full view of the camera.

'They do wash them before they send them out, don't they?' I asked hopefully.

The going was easier once we left the enduro course. This was a good dirt road, leading down to another steep section of woodland bisected by a river that a hundred years earlier had been used by the logging companies to float timber down to the sawmills. I'd seen a similar kind of thing in Alaska. They'd build dams across a gorge to let the water rise high enough to load it up, then tear down the dam and watch the logs bob downriver to where they would be gathered at the mills.

Denis took me through thick woodland to a spot where we could catch a glimpse of the gorge below. He described how when it was time to break up the dam, runners would ride the timber all the way down to the mill. Men with poles would walk the logs as they made their journey, shifting from one to another, fixing jams and making sure the timber ran freely. I imagined peeling off a rolling log and falling into the water with the weight of all that wood on top of you. With nobody to help you and a swift current like that, you'd be drowned in a heartbeat. That was a different time, when men risked their lives in this kind of country every day.

There was no logging here now; this was a recreational spot where people liked to swim and go gorge-jumping in the summer – sometimes hundreds of feet into the water below. Rather them than me, I thought.

We were soon back on the bikes and splitting the countryside in half, with rolling hills on one side and farmland on the other, the farmhouses built from white clapboard with massive Dutch barns in the yards. A little further on we stopped in a forest that was littered with what looked like electric cabling. I'd never seen anything like it; a spider's web interweaving the tree trunks throughout the whole forest. Suddenly it dawned on me: they were maple trees and the sap was being collected to make syrup. We were still out of season, so the pipes were not actually tapped into the wood; in season they are connected to a different hole every time the syrup is harvested; each hole is drilled a certain distance from the previous one and that way the tree remains unharmed. According to Denis one tree can produce sap for decades with no damage done whatsoever.

The drained sap is collected in massive steel drums and taken to what Denis called a boiling evaporator. There it's heated to a certain temperature, at which most of it just evaporates – what's left is maple syrup. It takes forty litres of sap to make one litre of maple syrup, and there are no additives, no preservatives and no process other than the cooking. I had no idea that that's how it came about. Maple syrup is one hundred per cent pure and it comes from these very trees. I gave the tree a hug. 'Thank you,' I said. 'Thank you, thank you. Without your maple syrup, I don't know where I'd be.'

Once we'd said goodbye to the guys and the bikes, we headed into Bathurst, New Brunswick, to jump on an overnight train to Quebec City. It was modern and we each had a very clean cabin, no bigger than a small cell but comfortable enough. Sitting down on the bed, I took a moment to reflect on the previous week. It was without doubt one of the nicest and most varied I'd spent in a long time, and I felt that we were starting to get to know the real Canada – we hadn't rushed through anything or anywhere.

I was beginning to realise that this is a very special country: there's a kindness in Canada, a tangible sense of courtesy among the people that I've not come across anywhere else. And I was really impressed that so many of those we'd met made their living from working the land or sea in the same way their forefathers had when they first came here. Next stop was Quebec, and I figured that ought to be an eye-opener for sure.

If you've never been to Quebec City, you really should visit. It has to be one of the most spectacular places I've ever seen. Early the next morning we were on the Funicular, climbing up from the lower part of the city: it's a sort of railway-cum-cable-car and the views across the multicoloured rooftops and the St Lawrence River are amazing. This was a different part of Canada altogether: the Capitale-Nationale region, French-speaking and the second largest of Quebec's cities after Montreal.

Hopping out of the Funicular, we met up with Sharon Frenette, a local guide who promised to show us some of the old parts of this place. As Quebec City is the only walled city on the North American continent, I was sure she'd have some good tales to tell. Sharon told us that the province was founded by the French in 1608, right on the St Lawrence

River, the gateway to North America. It was of vital strategic interest to both the French and the British, and the latter tried to invade on five separate occasions, which is why walls were built to defend the city. Unfortunately they were far from finished when the British army, under General Wolfe, arrived again in May of 1759. Initially he tried to attack from the eastern side, but the French were waiting, and by September the British still hadn't achieved their goal. On the night of 12 September, however, they managed to move 4,500 men up a dried-up stream bed to a place known to the Quebecois as the Plains of Abraham.

The story goes that at six o'clock the following morning, a French soldier raced to the city to tell his commanding officer that an army was on the Plains. The officer told him he'd had too much to drink and to go back to bed. In the end they had to send a second messenger from the watch to confirm what the first guy was saying, and word eventually reached the leader of the French forces, General Montcalm, that the enemy had indeed scaled the cliffs and were minutes from the city itself.

For sixty-three days the British had bombarded Quebec, leaving only a single house standing, but they had not been able to break down the walls. They were brutal, burning every farm within a hundred miles, hoping that that would force the militiamen to leave the city and go home to check on their families. It did, depleting the French army and leaving them so enraged that when they found their enemy on the Plains, they came tearing across like a horde of barbarians. The British waited calmly, and when the French were within thirty yards, General Wolfe gave the order to fire. The volley of musket balls tore into the oncoming troops, killing hundreds in their tracks. It was so intense that it took seven minutes for the smoke to clear enough for a second volley. By the time the third round had been fired, the French were fleeing. The battle lasted barely fifteen minutes and yet both the commanding generals were killed. The last thing that General Wolfe heard was someone crying, 'Look at that, the French are retreating!' He knew he would die a military hero. As for Montcalm, on his deathbed he stated that he was happy to die because now he would not have to see his precious Quebec under British rule. There's a monument to both men in Quebec with an inscription written in Latin so as not to offend either country. That seems like a mad kind of sensitivity when you consider they spent months knocking seven bells out of each other.

I was really interested to find out from Sharon how the Quebecois had managed to keep their identity, given that they spent so long under British rule.

'Ah,' she said. 'Of course the British wanted them all to be proper British citizens. No more Catholic Church, no more

French language, no more French law. But then they were already worrying about the American colonies. They were conscious that if the Americans decided to come up and attack Quebec, they would have the French on their side. So King George passed the Quebec Act, which allowed the people to retain their religion, language and code of law. And when, in 1775, the Americans finally did attack, the French helped you guys defeat them.'

Entente cordiale then, only not quite. Sharon told me that before the British finally left and the city returned to French rule, they lowered the walls by twenty feet just in case they wanted to come back some day and conquer it again.

After our history lesson, we went walkabout. What a place! It's so European, which was all the more noticeable after the colonial architecture we'd seen on the islands. It was like being in Paris – stone walls and turreted towers and people speaking French in shops and cafés. Walking the walls, we ducked into the old jail under what is now a library. Some of the cells are still there – tiny stone holes with an iron gate across the doorway. I took a quick look inside one of them but found myself locked in when the guard, Maxim, closed the gate, switched off the light and then secured the wooden door.

Solitary confinement for thirty days, that was what this cell had been used for. My God, it was dark. I've never experienced anything like it – it was horrendous. Maxim told me that if I really was there for thirty days I'd soon begin to lose all concept of time, and after a couple of weeks I'd begin to lose my mind. Yeah, I can see how that would happen: time to open up now, please. *Will someone open the door?*

Above the jail is a square room that's dominated by a statue of General Wolfe, sculpted in wood by the Chaulette brothers in 1779. The British didn't like the statue because it was a little short in stature, and of course the French didn't like it because it was the guy who'd conquered their city. So they didn't really care when two drunken ex-soldiers kidnapped it and took it across the Atlantic, where for three years it stood as the sign outside a pub. Finally somebody figured out what it was and eventually it was shipped back here.

I was sorry to leave Quebec City; it's definitely somewhere I will go back to. But it was time to hit the road once more, because Russ had something special lined up for me further north at the Saguenay Fjord.

We took the bridge across the St Lawrence that's a copy of Scotland's Forth Rail Bridge, only this one is all road. The

Canadians were adamant that the Quebec Bridge ought to be bigger than the Scottish one, and it is, although only by a metre. It took them a while to get it right, mind you; I was told that when they were building it, the construction collapsed on three separate occasions.

The Saguenay – which means windy river – drains from Lac Saint-Jean, a beautiful mountain lake surrounded by fir and spruce trees: a hotspot for city-dwellers wanting to get away. There are all sorts of things you can do up here – sailing, kayaking, swimming – but I was meeting up with a mountain guide who was going to lead me up the Via Ferrata, which is Italian for 'Iron Way', to do some rock-climbing.

There is a rock face on one side of the lake that's been fitted with an iron cable hammered in with pitons. It's actually a traverse rather than a climb, and my guide, Wade, told me the cable was there to help us hang on for dear life above the raging water. 'Right,' I said, 'so I can be like Sylvester Stallone, then, in that movie *Cliffhanger*?'

He looked me up and down. 'I think you're missing a little . . . you know . . . muscle there, feller, you know what I mean?'

He took me to the gear hut so we could suit up with safety harness, karabiners and helmets. It's always a bit worrying when you have to wear all this equipment, and I can't deny I was feeling just a touch queasy. It's all very well being the front man on these expeditions, but you're also the guy who has to do the dangerous stuff. I checked out the whistle Wade had given me for attracting attention. Yep, it worked: good. I was bound to need it. He told me that nobody had ever fallen to their death from the Via Ferrata, but there's always a first time for everything.

Wade then proceeded to tell me the three options now available to this intrepid Chris Bonington wannabe: easy, medium and extreme. I didn't like the sound of that last one, but I also knew that Russ or Mungo was about to remind me of the title of the programme, so before they could show me up for the coward I just might be, I said: 'Let's go extreme!'

We were high on a cliff overlooking the water, and with a nervous laugh I admitted to Wade that I thought I might have lost my mojo.

'Your mojo?' he said. 'Brother, *now* is not the time to lose your mojo.'

From the clifftop, we began to make our way down a series of steep steps in the rock, with the iron cable guiding us. It was then that I made the mistake of looking down. Bloody hell, that was a bit of a drop! Although the water wasn't coursing as much as I had feared, it was still slapping the base of the rocks like the waves at Cape Spear. Thank God

I was clipped on to that cable. I knew that if I slipped, the harness would keep me from falling, but I would still hang ignominiously, scrabbling at the wall. Despite my fears, however, I gradually started to enjoy it, even getting a little cocky – holding on to the great iron grips fixed into the rock while swapping my feet around like a dancer. Then it was into an overhang, where a length of four-by-four had been fitted as there were no footholds. There were no handholds here either, only polished rock or the option of clinging on to the cable itself. It didn't feel very safe. Taking a moment to have a breather and inspect the bloodied calluses on my hands, I clipped the spare karabiner on to a metal loop and leant back. Suddenly I heard something crack and almost soiled my pants. 'Jesus!' I cried. 'What was that?' One of the boards we were walking on had creaked, ominously, as Russ stepped on it. I desperately screwed the thread on that second karabiner so it couldn't work itself loose by mistake.

Despite a few panicky moments, the whole thing was great fun – though it was a little awkward trying to film with Nat on the line with me, Mungo above and Russ behind us taking photos. It was the perfect way to view the stunning countryside, and finally we'd been blessed with a beautiful day – warm and sunny, with only a light wind. As we rested on a perch on the cliffside, Lac Saint-Jean was an expanse of shimmering water before us; sitting there with the sun on my face, I really did feel like I was hidden away from the rest of the world.

My moment of solitude didn't last for long, though – what Wade had planned for me next was anything but hidden away. The extreme high-ropes course. 'It's designed to challenge you, Charley,' he said. 'And I mean *challenge* you.'

Between us, climbing into the heavens, was a vertically hanging log with wooden pegs hammered into it at various intervals. 'This is the ladder of natural selection,' Wade said. 'You're familiar with the theory of evolution?'

'Sure,' I said, cautiously.

'Well, this is going to determine whether you keep evolving or fall way behind.'

'How do I get up it?' I asked. 'Or do I have to figure that out for myself?'

You've got it. I had to figure it out for myself. So, using the harness and karabiners, I clipped into the metal protection loops that studded my ascent and laboriously made my way from peg to peg.

'Is it hard?' Russ called from below.

I looked down at him, one eyebrow cocked. 'More a pain in the arse actually, mate. More a pain in the arse.'

It was knackering: one arm wrapped around the log while trying to move the karabiners from ring to ring.

Wade was no help. 'Come on, Charley,' he called. 'If you're not able to get to the top, you have to go back to the family ropes course.'

You just had to love this guy, didn't you? Undeterred, I climbed on and finally made it to a wooden platform, where I could pause to catch my breath, though not for very long. Now I had a tightrope walk to perform – a cable extending between the treetops with another at shoulder height to clip on to. Like some high-wire walker from a circus, with the crowd cheering me on from below, I set out, sliding one foot and then the other along the cable. I made it, just, heart in my mouth. At the far platform I clung on to the tree as if my life depended on it. Fortunately I didn't have to go back the way I'd come – there was a regular wooden-rung rope ladder to descend.

On terra firma once more, I was sweating like a pig when Wade came up with another impossible task. 'OK,' he said. 'For this next bit we're free from our karabiners and you can jump, dive and struggle your way across.' Gesturing with the kind of enthusiasm only the most sadistic torturers display, he rattled on, 'You jump off the platform, try to grab hold of that first hanging pyramid, bear-hug it, get as high up as you can, then reach for the next one and swing yourself from one to the next.' Pausing for breath he added, 'It's impossible for an ordinary man, but from what I've seen today, I think you'll be able to handle it.'

I stared at him, wondering if Ewan wasn't paying him or something, getting me back for all those sand dunes we'd had to ride across on *Long Way Down*. Below me was a net, of course, but I still wasn't convinced I could do it without falling. I wondered what I was doing here; if I'd wanted to be a trapeze artist I'd have run away and joined the circus, wouldn't I?

I think I made it to the first pyramid and that was it. I peeled off and lay on my back with the net supporting me, just trying to catch my breath. That had to be it now, didn't it? But no, they were not done with me yet. Next I was clipped on to a single cable with a series of hanging rungs to cross and the forest floor far, far below. By this point I reckon my blood pressure was through the roof, and I was hanging on to the overhead cable for dear life, wavering around on the wooden rungs that bobbed under my feet. They were wobbling so much I could barely get from one to the next. Why didn't I just have a normal job? I wondered. You know, one where the alarm goes off and you pack your lunch and drive off to work listening to the radio. I was exhausted and beaten up to the point where my legs felt like hunks of immovable lead.

After acting like some sort of partially evolved ape for the past few hours, I was delighted to finally don a life jacket, grab a paddle and head out on to the lake. Saguenay is a playground, it really is, and the fun doesn't stop when the snow comes; it just shifts to ice-fishing, snowmobiling and dog-sledding. You name it, they do it at Saguenay.

It wasn't long before we found the most amazing waterfall: gallons and gallons flowing over a pinnacle of rock. Now we're talking. Paddling right up close, I finally washed the sweat from my aching body by diving in. God, it was cold! Saguenay is a glacial mountain lake and it only sees the sun for three months of the year. That didn't stop me. The adrenalin must still have been pumping, because I swam the width of the falls then climbed on to the rocks and stepped beyond the torrent, feeling like Daniel Day-Lewis in *The Last of the Mohicans*. Eventually the wall of water swept me off the rocks and the others hauled me back into the boat.

'OK, Hawkeye,' Russ said. 'I think that's enough for today.'

4

Something Cold
and Something Blue

Saguenay really reminded me of *Deliverance*, the film my dad directed years ago with Burt Reynolds and Jon Voight: the water, the rapids, the way the woodland comes down to the shore. I had really enjoyed exploring the place. But after a crazy few days, it was time to take a breather in Toronto before the next stage of this epic journey.

Our few days of R&R meant I had a chance to visit the bike shop on Yonge Street in downtown Toronto. The previous night we'd been to the MMVA music awards ceremony – there's a huge music scene in Canada, Toronto especially, which is partially supported by grants, ensuring that Canada retains a separate artistic identity from that of the United States. We'd met a cool guy called Nathan with a great mop of curly black hair, who played in a band called Midway State, and spent much of the evening trying to persuade him to do the music for the TV show. He'd been a fan of *Long Way Round* and joined me at the shop to get a feel for the bikes. I suggested he hop on the back and we'd do a couple of blocks of Yonge Street; it's the longest street in the world, according to the *Guinness Book of Records*, running from the shores of Lake Ontario all the way to Rainy River, 1,896 kilometres further north. Nathan had never even swung a leg over a bike before but he soon got the hang of it. We cruised the streets for a while, and when we were done he said he'd work on some music for us.

After saying goodbye to Nathan, we set off up Yonge Street, aiming for the Fathom Five dive site in Tobermory, which is regarded as the scuba-diving capital of Canada. As I'd spent so much time hanging from a rope above water, I thought it was time to get below the surface. Pulling in to Tobermory four hours later, we stopped at a shop called Divers Den, where I met Mike, a young guy in a polo shirt, who was to be our dive master for the afternoon. He was going to take us to the wreck of the *Niagara II*, a steel-hulled ship that had been sunk deliberately in 1999 for the enjoyment of divers. He told me we could dive inside the wreck itself and swim up through the smokestack. It sounded awesome, although apparently the water was going to be pretty cold.

'So, it'll be peeing in the wetsuit to keep warm, then?' I said.

'Only if *you* want to wash it, Charley,' he told me.

In total, twenty-five ships had been wrecked within a five-kilometre radius at Tobermory, and I was delighted when Mike said we could also dive on *The Sweepstakes*, a much older boat that had foundered in a storm in Big Tub Harbour back in 1901.

While I'd been talking, Russ had been out back suiting up, and he came through flexing his biceps like the Adonis he clearly is. I'm not sure how he was feeling, but I was a tad anxious. I've dived a few times in my life, but never in fresh water, where the visibility isn't so good, and never in cold water. I knew this was going to be very, very cold, and my fears were not allayed when they gave me *three* wetsuits to put on.

As I grabbed a couple of air bottles and hauled them aboard the boat, the skipper blasted out an old sea shanty to get us in the mood. I danced along to the music, no doubt looking like an overstuffed seal. Just in case you haven't been following on the map, we were on Lake Huron, which is the second largest of the Great Lakes and the third largest freshwater lake in the world. It's named after the Huron Indians, part of the Iroquois Confederacy. Contrary to popular belief, they rather than the Mohicans were the ones with the 'Mohawk' hairstyle.

Leaving the dock behind, we hugged the coastline until we were over the first dive site, where Mike began his safety briefing. All he kept talking about was the cold.

'I want to make sure you guys are adding air to your vests while you're going down,' he stated. 'Try not to do it while you're breathing in, because I want to avoid a reg freeze-up at the bottom. As I said, this is extreme cold diving.'

You see? All I'd done was Indonesia and the Caribbean, where I barely needed a wetsuit – now it was *extreme* cold diving.

Russ was listening carefully. 'What's a reg freeze-up?' he asked.

'Well,' Mike said, 'in cold water if there's too much air going through the first stage of the regulator it can freeze up, which means you'll be getting air all the time. That means your tank isn't going to last very long, and we want to avoid that so you can have as long as possible under water.'

We got the rest of the gear on – rubber helmets, tanks and fins – and were ready to make the descent. On the steps at the dive platform I covered my mask and dropped in. Bloody hell, that's cold, I thought. Holy shite, that isn't cold – it's *freezing*.

Forty-two degrees Fahrenheit, which in our language is about eight degrees. The breath seemed to stop in my throat. It was really unnerving, and this was only on the surface. God knows what it was going to be like when we went below. I could not shut up. I kept on and on about how cold it was, while on deck Mungo and Nat were killing themselves laughing. 'Funniest diving I've ever seen! That's backstroke, Charley,' Mungo called. 'Don't be such a wuss, mate. Get below!'

The trouble was, I didn't feel comfortable. I couldn't get my breath, my chest was so tight I thought I was having a panic attack and I found myself clinging on to the rope attached to the buoy that marked the position of the wreck. Mike was giving me a pep talk while I tried to calm down and do something about my breathing.

'Are you all right?' he called to Russ, who was behind me and actually hanging on to the buoy itself now.

'No,' Russ admitted. 'I can't seem to get a breath.'

We had to get it together: this was extreme frontiers and we couldn't just quit. Eventually we managed to go under, and submerged at last we made our way down the rope, hand over hand, from the buoy to the shipwreck a few fathoms below. I've never had a panic attack in my life, but the feeling was still close, and it wasn't helped by the fact that I kept having to clear the skin-chapping water from my mask.

At last though, we were on the wreck. I stood on deck, where a Canadian flag fluttered languidly, listening to the sound of my own breathing. Moments later I was diving through the engine room deep into the bowels of the ship before ascending the height of the smokestack. Russ was ahead of me, and there was something eerie about being in that tunnel of darkness watching his fins fan the water into the light above. We passed through open doorways, peered through gaping portholes; I found an old enamel mug and pretended to drink from it. We dived inside the wheelhouse, into the living quarters still with their tables and bunks. It was amazing to realise that once upon a time people had been living and working here. Despite the fact that I knew this vessel had been sunk deliberately, I couldn't help but think of the *Titanic* and all those headstones I'd seen in Halifax. I tried to imagine night-time on the lake, with the weather storming; I thought of being on a sinking ship with no one to call for help and feeling the first freezing bite as you leapt overboard with no hope of making it to safety.

I don't know why, but on the way up I started to feel panicky all over again. I'd been all right on the bottom, but now I couldn't breathe properly. I don't like the feeling of my face being enclosed, which is why I prefer to have an open-face motorcycle helmet. There was something unbelievably claustrophobic suddenly about wearing a dive helmet. On the way back to the boat I had to pull the rubber mask off so I could breathe. I've never experienced anything quite like it before. It felt as if the life was being sucked out of my face.

Both Russ and I felt a real sense of accomplishment having dived in temperatures like that. It's not for the faint-hearted and at the beginning neither of us thought we were going to be able to make it. As Russ came on deck we shook hands. 'I tell you what,' he said as he stripped off his tank. 'I've been to some places in the world with you, Charley, but down there, standing by the ship's wheel, I thought, that's as good a place to have been together as any I could think of.'

By the time we were out of our wetsuits and gliding over the top of the sunken *Sweepstakes*, I wasn't in the mood for getting wet again. We could see all the wrecks from the boat, just below the surface in some places. This really was wreck city; no wonder it was the scuba-diving capital of the country. Mike pointed out a wreck from the late 1800s – at one time you could dive inside it, make your way the length of the hull and come out at the other end. They'd stopped that now, though, separating each section with cages because divers left a trail of air bubbles that became trapped in the wreck and accelerated the rotting process. Russ commented that the wooden wrecks were in good condition and that had to have something to do with the timber they used, because fresh water rots wood just as badly as salt water does.

I was back in my street clothes, but Russ was going in again. 'Good luck, mate,' I said. 'I'll see you back here in time for the ice hockey.'

5

Messing About on the Ice

Ice hockey is Canada's most popular spectator sport – although they just call it 'hockey' – and we were off to train with one of its legends, Reggie Leach. Reggie is an indigenous, or First Nations, Canadian who had a long and distinguished career in the National Hockey League (which also covers the USA) back in the 1970s, playing for various teams including the Boston Bruins and the Philadelphia Flyers, with whom he won the prestigious Stanley Cup. Reggie was a serious player, the Wayne Rooney of 1970s ice hockey; in one season he scored sixty-one goals, notching up nineteen in the play-offs alone. His record still stands. I wondered if that made him a little nervous at the beginning of each season, but he pointed out that records are meant to be broken and that sooner or later somebody was going to come along and do just that. I'd heard that kind of talk before: John McGuinness with his TT records, Giacomo Agostini, the most successful motorcycle racer in history, with more Grand Prix wins than anyone else, they all claim that records are there to be broken, but I bet there's a bit of every great champion that really hopes theirs won't be. After all, it's that kind of winning mentality that made them a champion in the first place.

Reggie now works with First Nations kids, teaching them how to play hockey. I met him at the T.M. Davies arena in a town called Lively, and before I knew it he had me in the changing room getting kitted out. First I had to slide on a pair of Lycra pants with a massive codpiece at the front. I felt like Blackadder, the way it was dangling, and I made a great show of prancing around the changing room.

Once Reggie had helped me with the inner pants, I put on the rest of the kit. The body armour the players wear under their shirts is lightweight and close-fitting; even a guy with my physique ends up looking like some sort of Roman gladiator. On top went a baggy shirt, and the whole thing was finished off with a helmet and, of course, skates. Reggie looked impressed – not with the way I was turned out, necessarily, but with what he called my 'play-off beard'. Apparently the goatee I've cultivated over the years is exactly what the players who reach the play-offs grow for the occasion, only in their case they keep it going until their team gets knocked out. The teams that reach the finals often have guys on the ice with full beards, because once they start growing, it's bad luck to shave them off.

Oh, wow. I was so looking forward to this, although I wasn't exactly feeling confident. Reggie was going to put me through my paces with a bunch of kids, the youngest of whom was about seven years old. Seven. That's nearly thirty (ish) years my junior and this bore all the hallmarks of potential humiliation. I'd played field hockey when I was at school, but Mungo didn't think it would help much.

The kids were all whizzing about as if they'd been born on the bloody ice and all I could do was try and keep up. I was nervous – ice hockey is the fastest team sport in the world, and if you've seen it, you'll know there is *always* a fist fight and the refs rarely get involved. It wasn't fist fights I was worried about right then, however; it was getting around. I'm not bad on roller blades, but on the ice – kitted out like the Incredible Hulk and with a hockey stick and the puck to worry about too – I was slipping and sliding all over the place.

The basics of the training involved 'carrying' the puck around the circles on the ice and shooting at the goal. By carrying, Reggie meant working it from side to side with the stick, moving in a circle. Having Reggie there to coach was a help, and I began to get better. I'd been doing it one-handed, but that was all wrong – you needed two hands on the stick at all times, and Reggie insisted I learn how to carry the puck properly. The most important thing he told me was that far from being a hindrance, the stick was actually a help. He showed me how to use it to balance, and I started to get the hang of it, skating over the ice, working the puck from side to side before I let fly and hammered it beyond the goaltender. A goal! I'd scored a goal! Of course I celebrated like a true pro, sliding across the ice on my belly to smack up against Mungo's knees.

Really, I wasn't half bad ... in a sprint for the puck with a seven-year-old boy I came second, which, despite the fact that there were only two of us, wasn't that terrible. Yes, I was a little slower than the kids, but I was in control, sort of. I did spend quite a bit of time on my knees, and that was before we started going backwards. Again it was a child half my size who showed me the way, easing his skates back and forth behind him and dragging the puck along. He made it look so simple, and yet when I had a go I sort of shuffled and fell again.

Reggie tried to offer some encouragement by telling me that the seven-year-old who'd whipped my butt in the sprint had been skating since he was about three and was now one of the top players in the area for his age. That was all right then, at least I had an excuse. The girls were all better than me as well – up until the age of thirteen they trained with the boys, so I imagined they could hold their own in a fist fight.

One of the most difficult exercises was working the puck around a cone signifying another player. That was when I went down the hardest. I tried again and again and kept hitting the ice with my chin no matter what. The difficulty was moving from a forward motion to a backward one after pivoting on the skates. We played a mock game and I did all right, though I fell over quite a bit. By the time we were finished I really was exhausted. I'd completely lost all my energy and these kids were skating rings around me. Before I'd gone out on the ice I'd had no idea how energy-sapping it would be. Reggie told me that when he was a professional player he used to go to training camp to get in shape for the season, whereas now the pro players have to be in shape just to get to the training camp. He reckoned the pro players would spend forty minutes every day working on those sprints alone, again and again and again. Though Reggie never claimed to be the fittest player on the circuit, he could score goals – it's a bit like in football, I suppose; there are those players who just seem to have the knack. And Reggie most certainly did; his shots were clocked at an average speed of 115 miles an hour, so fast the goaltender could barely see the puck, never mind save it. What really blew me away, though, was that when Reggie was playing you didn't have to wear a helmet – that rule didn't come in until 1980. I took a moment to think about it: being hit in the head by a puck at over a hundred miles an hour. I doubted you'd come out alive.

These kids were just one of several groups Reggie coached. He told me that many First Nations parents encourage their children to play hockey, not necessarily because they have grand designs on the kids becoming NHL players in the future, but because they want to give them a focus, to keep them out of trouble. There's a drink and drug problem among youngsters in Canada just as there is anywhere else, but the fitness requirements of hockey alone would help prevent them getting into that. In his own youth Reggie made lots of mistakes – he had a serious drink problem – and his goal now is to pass on some of what he has learned to his people, to give them a sense of purpose regardless of whether it leads to the professional game. He has lots to teach them; not only his hockey skills, but also the resolve to overcome life's difficulties. He told me he'd joined Alcoholics Anonymous in 1985 and had been on the wagon ever since.

I really liked Reggie, and although becoming a professional ice-hockey player has had to be scrubbed off my list of unfulfilled ambitions, I learned a lot, and not just about the game. Reggie is one of those cool people who, although he had plenty of talent, knows how fortunate he was, and has spent his life since retiring trying to give something back.

It was a welcome relief to be back on a bike the next day. We were travelling first to Winnipeg then to Thunder Bay, where we would hook up with some guides from Northern Soul Wilderness Adventures, who were taking us on a river trip.

We were still riding along Yonge Street, and plugging the coordinates into the GPS, when I discovered we had six hundred kilometres ahead of us. We'd already ridden eight hundred on Yonge Street since Toronto. One of these days I'm going to do all nineteen hundred, maybe with my wife Ollie and the kids.

So it was back on the highway, with the railway and a massive freight train on my left and the tarmac unravelling under the wheels. The Atlantic was behind me and the Rocky Mountains ahead. So far the only boundary we had pushed was the Atlantic, and that left both the south and the north before we rolled into Vancouver. We passed through small towns beyond which the land seemed flat and featureless, and the traffic grew less and less until it seemed I was the only person out there. It was mind-blowing to think I'd been on the same stretch of highway all the way from Toronto. I was contented, really deep-down happy. This was my signature, it was what I did: the road unwinding as I winged my way west on a GS1200 with off-road tyres, panniers and top box.

The weather was rubbish, though; since Toronto it had been raining pretty much non-stop, and that kind of damp can get you down. It didn't let up either; when we woke the following morning, the sky was still a mass of black rain clouds and it was cold outside. With the river trip coming up, I was beginning to wonder if we'd get rained on the entire way. We had planned a couple of nights under canvas, which could be a complete disaster if this kept up. According to the news, Winnipeg had seen more rain than they'd had in years, and the farmers had been unable to plant their crops.

Having ridden through the rain the previous day and with all my energy having been sucked out of me by the ice hockey, I fancied just chilling for a while, so I wimped out, packed the bike in the trailer and decided to see if I could hitch a ride with Barry in his RV. Barry worked for Eagle Rider Motorcycles, who had transported the bikes, and he was there to make sure we had back-up when we weren't riding. To Barry that RV was home, and he liked the fact that his home was portable. Except this morning, the morning I'd asked if I could have a lift, it didn't seem so portable after all. The batteries were flat – all six of them – and Barry spent a large part of the morning trying to get it figured out, while I kicked my heels in the parking lot. Finally the sun came out and I decided I didn't want the lift after all.

I seemed to regain all my strength, and suddenly riding was all I could think about. It had nothing to do with the problems with the RV – this was the first day in a week when the sun had been shining, and I wasn't going to let that go by. With many miles still to cover, the best way to do it was on two wheels, and all at once I was desperate to get under way. So off I went again, and with the sky blue and the sun overhead, I could've ridden all day. In fact we arrived in Winnipeg in the late afternoon. Passing under the railroad bridge, we followed the signs north for Main Street, where we'd been booked into the Fort Garry Hotel. From the outside it looked innocuous enough, but inside was reputedly the most haunted hotel room in North America. Room 202. Guess which room Russ had booked me into for tonight?

I hate all that stuff, really I do. I mean, what was he thinking? I can't even watch horror movies and he knows that. But this trip was about pushing the boundaries, and not just physically I suppose, so I had no choice. Having said that, it really was a very nice hotel, palatial in fact, and we weren't paying. We'd been on a very tight budget the whole trip, and this night's rest – if I was to get any rest in this haunted room – was courtesy of the Canadians. I guess they wanted to see how I would fare in Room 202.

The Fort Garry was built in 1913 by the Grand Trunk Pacific Railway, and is only a block from Winnipeg's Union Station. Those railway entrepreneurs were certainly canny; they didn't just create a method of getting from coast to coast, they cornered the market in places to stay along the way. Anyway, against my better judgement I checked into Room 202 while the manager, Paul, filled me in on what I might expect. He told me that many guests had seen the ghost of a young woman (which was better than some demonic monster, I suppose, although not much). Apparently after only one day of wedded bliss, her husband had been killed in a car crash and, devastated by grief, his young widow had hanged herself in the closet of the room I'd just been allocated: oh joy and happy days.

As Paul took me up there, he told me it was not a popular room; apart from at Halloween, people who knew the history actively avoided it. The widow had been spotted at the end of the bed and two maids claimed to have seen blood seeping from the walls, which for someone like me was about as bad as it can get. Only a couple of months ago, a young woman had wanted her picture taken by the door of Room 202, but her camera wouldn't work. Moving down the corridor to Room 208 she tried again and the camera was fine, so she went back to 202. Guess what? Yes, the camera failed again.

The corridor was like any other in this kind of upmarket hotel: nicely carpeted and quiet, you know the sort of thing. Room 202 was right at the end beside the fire doors, beyond which there was a staircase, so that was one escape route at least. Paul gave a little knock just to make sure the widow was aware we were coming in and then he unlocked the door.

I was chewing my nails, trying to look cool and calm but not doing a very good job. The room was not the best in the hotel, but it was nicely decorated. I tried to tell myself it was just a room. A room where a woman had committed suicide.

'Anyway,' Paul said. 'I'll wish you good night. Hopefully there will be no disturbances. Oh,' he added, 'and don't be like the last person who stayed here, will you.'

'Why?' I asked. 'What happened to them?'

'He ran out of the hotel at two thirty in the morning.'

'You're joking?'

He shook his head. 'No, I'm not. He ran out with his shirt tail hanging out, kicking his suitcase ahead of him in an absolute panic.'

I was incredulous now. 'What happened?'

'He woke up in bed and the room was freezing cold; for about forty-five seconds he couldn't move, he couldn't even blink. When I spoke to him he was white as a sheet, and he told me that lying there like that, he knew there was somebody else in the room. He hadn't been drinking, he was just a regular guy, but he hated the feeling he got in this room so he upped and left in the middle of the night.' He smiled now, encouragingly. 'Anyway, good night, Charley. Sleep well, won't you.'

I didn't unpack. I sat in the chair by the window and rocked. I had Mungo with me, filming just in case the widow appeared. We sat around, taking the piss, messing about – Mungo pointed out that me being there was definitely going to stir the widow up, rile her, stuff like that. On top of it all we had to be up at five thirty for the three-hour drive to meet up with the guides for the Bloodvein River trip. Bloodvein. God, that was appropriate, wasn't it?

6

River Wild

She didn't bother me. She must've liked me, because I did sleep and I didn't wake up at two thirty, screaming and shouting and rushing down to 207 and Russ's double bed. I was so knackered after the two-day ride and the ice hockey that I crashed out and didn't stir until the alarm went off. I jumped out of bed, ready to board a floatplane for our trip into the wilderness.

When we arrived in Bissett, our guide Cameron White and his team were busy overseeing exactly what we were taking on the floatplane. We'd each been allocated a watertight barrel for our belongings and these were loaded into the fuselage.

'Make sure you've packed everything you're going to

need,' Cam told us, 'because if you haven't, this is going to be a bad trip.'

'Like toilet paper, you mean?' I asked.

'Right . . . or food maybe. It would be an idea to take food. Having said that, we could always survive on fish – it's good where we're going because people don't go there to fish. Now I come to think about it, people don't really go there at all.'

There were four guides in all: Cam, Rob, Dave and Matt. Four boats, two men to a boat, and we each needed to be with someone who had some experience. We also had to make sure we were not exceeding the floatplane's payload. It could only carry so much, and only two canoes at a time, which meant we'd be making two trips. Russ and Nat were going ahead, then the pilot would turn around and come back for Mungo and me. We'd driven three hours north of Winnipeg already this morning and now the plane was going to fly us fifty miles further. Last night when Russ and I had plotted the route on the map, we'd realised that we really would be in the middle of nowhere.

With the gear loaded, the pilot began the very delicate process of strapping the canoes on to the struts above the plane's floats. It had to be done very carefully because we didn't want them coming loose and falling off. He told us that if a canoe did come off it would probably take the tail section and us along with it.

'Would it?' Russ gave me a quick glance. 'That's heartening.'

Finally the plane was ready and Russ and Nat climbed in. 'Good luck, guys,' I called. 'See you up there.' We watched as it took off, bumping across the flattened surface of the lake and then into the air until the sound died and it was nothing more than a speck on the horizon.

An hour and a half later it was my turn. With two more canoes strapped on, Mungo and I climbed aboard and I took my seat alongside the pilot. The plane was pretty roomy actually, although very basic, with the seats in the back little more than benches along the sides. We were in the air for about thirty minutes before I could make out the Bloodvein River cutting through the landscape below us, just like an artery. This was like nothing I'd ever seen before, not a hint of humanity as far as the eye could make out. I was really excited now. Cam had said we were going to a place nobody went to, and from the air you could tell that he meant it. All I could see was a vast expanse of forest bisected by the river and its tributaries. As we began the descent, I have to say my heart was in my mouth for a moment. I've flown small planes and landing is always the tricky bit, and this was a floatplane coming down on a narrow river with trees on both sides. It would be very easy to get this wrong. As we went lower, of course, that narrow strip of waterway became a lot wider, and our pilot knew what he was doing. He had a massive grin on his face and you could tell he just loved this bit. Checking the wind, he chose his spot and nose-dived into the canyon, pulling up to drop us on the water with barely a splash from the floats. Then we just cruised towards the bank and tied off. Really it was as simple as arriving on a boat.

Once the gear was unloaded, we were straight into the canoes. The plane headed upriver for a few hundred yards before the pilot brought it about and came hurtling down towards us, lifting off right over our heads. In a moment he would be gone and we'd be on our own: eight guys in four boats in the Manitoban wilderness. The canoes we were using were open kayaks – Canadian style with a single short paddle – a modern version of those used by the fur traders, or Voyageurs, who transported their goods by canoe all those years ago.

We rafted up (as Dave put it) for a moment or two; that was when all four boats come alongside each other so we could discuss what was going to happen next. As though he was somehow reluctant to leave us, the pilot made a pass overhead and performed a little wing wave before finally disappearing above the trees. Cam was busy giving us a short briefing: the plan was to paddle as far as the Akeeko Rapids and set up camp. 'OK,' he said, 'before we head off I'll give you some whistle information. If I blow my whistle once, it means listen up. If I blow twice, it means raft up. That's a position of safety: if we're all together like this, nothing's going to sink us, OK? If I blow my whistle three times, that means there's an emergency and we have to get to shore immediately. Everybody got that?'

It was a sombre and important moment, though I have to say I was busy showing Mungo the name tag I'd written on my paddle: 'Charley Big Boy'. You know it's true; you only have to ask my wife.

Paddling downriver, we took the left fork and a little further on we headed for shore just ahead of the rapids. Once the boats were pulled up and upturned, we strung lines of thin rope between the trees to clip our rucksacks on to. Another safety feature; we'd know where they were at all times, which was important, because if we lost anything it was the end of our journey.

A hint of white bone half hidden in the dirt caught the sun, and looking closer we saw it was a skull – quite a big skull actually, although Cam said it belonged to a small sturgeon. It was pretty savage-looking, but Cam reckoned it was all that remained of a catch an eagle had brought up. We were close to some slabs of stone that formed the entrance to the rapids, and in order to simulate what it would be like if one of us got tossed out of the boat, they got me to walk out and plunge in. Once in the running water, I had to lie on my back with my feet up and ankles together, my arms spread in a crucifix shape. That's the most efficient and safest way of riding the water, because your feet are a far better buffer for obstacles than your head. With your arms spread out you have the least amount of body mass under the water, so there's less chance that you'll snag on anything hidden below. Assuming the position, I rode the rapids to deeper water and was relieved to find that, unlike Lake Huron, the temperature was beautiful.

Following my lead, Russ rode down next but somehow whacked his coccyx on a rock – I reckon you could hear the yell all the way to Winnipeg. Nat and Mungo came down safely. Back at camp, Dave was cooking steak and potatoes with carrot and onion all fried in olive oil, and the smell was really enticing for a bunch of hungry explorers like us. After taking that early bath, some good food in the open air was just what the doctor ordered. The dining table was the hull of an upturned canoe and we were serenaded by the rapids as we ate. It was good eating, as they say, and I really felt like I'd earned it, driving up to Bissett, packing the gear, flying in and paddling, not to mention floating over the rapids.

When dinner was over, it was time for the plastic bag of toilet paper and the walk of shame; deep into the forest I went, reminding myself to be careful with my mobile phone.

The last thing I needed was to lose that to the waste pile, as had happened on camping trips in the past.

'Turn your mike off, Charley,' Nat called. 'We don't want the soundtrack from back here.'

It was an eventful first night: we were using hoop tents, where you don't need to put pegs in unless the weather is really bad. We'd gone to bed with the sky clear, so that was all right. Sometime later, though, I woke to howling winds, pouring rain and thunder. I leapt up, secured the tent and made sure all my stuff was inside and the tent was zipped against the gazillion mosquitoes that occupied the riverbank. I was nicely snuggled down in my sleeping bag again when I realised I'd forgotten to have a pee. Oh well, there was no way I was going to venture out again. Somehow I managed to make it through the night without the needs of my bladder overwhelming me.

Cam told me that Akeeko is a First Nations word that means 'kettle' – apparently because of kettle-shaped formations in the granite rocks bordering the rapids – and that these rapids were running at category four. That was too steep for the kind of open boats we were paddling, so, like the Voyageurs of old, we had to portage the canoes around them. Dave carried a canoe on his own; grabbing the central seat strut, he hauled its weight on to his thigh, then, with a bend of the knees, flipped it up and carried it over his head. I watched him make his way through the trees to the other side of the white water without any help. Then it was our turn, Russ and I taking an end apiece and walking it between us.

There was no livestock up here – no sheep to contaminate anything – so we filled our water bottles straight from the river, then sorted what we needed for the day into the waterproof bags we'd been given and prepared to get on our way. The gear barrels were sealed with a locking device that made sure they were watertight, even if one happened to go overboard. Fitted with a harness, they were carried like a backpack when you were ashore.

A good way downriver was the Bloodvein community, one of the First Nations villages, where we were due in a couple of days. I was looking forward to meeting the people. I've always had an interest in native cultures and met plenty of aboriginals on our trip to Australia a couple of years ago. In North America their story is as tragic as anywhere else, I suppose: they were subjugated and forcibly removed from their homelands. I knew a little of what had happened south of the border, but I wasn't sure how it had been up here. We'd find out in a couple of days, but in the meantime we had the river to negotiate.

We're going to need one hell of a big glass of whisky for this 20,000-year-old ice cube! Our trip on Dean and Dave's boat in Newfoundland was the perfect start to our Extreme Frontiers journey.

Racing towards the tidal bore on the Shubenacadie River, Nova Scotia, at full speed.

Lobster fishing in Nova Scotia with Merril McInnes and his family on the *Briton Cove Bounty*. It was an early start, but we were working too hard to appreciate the beautiful sunrise.

A beautiful specimen, perfect for feeding the crew back on dry land . . .

. . . and two not-quite-so-beautiful specimens.

That's my 'let's off-road' smile! Nothing I like better.

Off-roading on the dirt-bike. There was one corner which caught me out every time, but it was still great to be on the bike where I belong.

Look, no hands! Hanging around on the Via Ferrata, with Quebec's Saguenay Fjord below.

The aerial assault course was extreme, all right.

And after climbing, hanging, shuffling and balancing my way across a never-ending series of obstacles, it was definitely time for a little lie-down.

With the team (Nat, Mungo, me and Russ) at the beginning of the world's longest road, Yonge Street in Toronto. Only 1,898 kilometres to go.

On the ice with legendary hockey player Reggie Leach, in Lively, Ontario.

My teammates . . . the ones who skated rings around me.

Canoeing on the Bloodvein River in
Manitoba was definitely more
Deliverance than *Hawaii Five-O*.

Failing to pass muster as a cadet with the Royal Canadian Mounted Police. They must have been shining those shoes all night!

On the firing range with the Mounties. All police officers in Canada carry guns, although gun crime is much lower than it is in the United States.

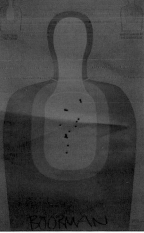

With Jay at the Atlas No. 3 mine near Drumheller in Alberta. I was happy to be up in the fresh air after the confined spaces of the coal mine.

Working up to a full head of steam on board Linda, the engine used to bring the coal out from the mine.

I loved finding out about the dinosaurs at the Royal Tyrrell Museum of Palaeontology in Drumheller. This was serious scientific stuff, but of course I found the time to mess around.

Suited up in helmets and PFDs (personal floating devices), we were finally under way. We had to be wary. The open-style canoe is quite tippy; it's easy to unbalance the thing and they have to be packed very carefully to get the distribution of weight just right. As Cam and I rode that first eddy, I remembered someone once telling me that there's only one rule in canoeing, and that is 'paddle or die'. There was a lot to remember. We fairly flew downstream, though; the current was swift in this section, and keeping a bank of teeth-like rocks to our left, we rode the waves to the point.

The beauty of the way we were travelling was twofold: two people in a craft like this brings challenges you don't get if you float down a river on a raft; you have to work in unison. The other thing is that the canoe is much smaller than a raft and it can get you places that a bigger vessel cannot. I have to say it also felt less like fun and much more like the kind of expedition the first explorers of this waterway would have made. As Cam pointed out, the rivers have been the highways of this part of Canada for as long as people have been here. Before the Europeans arrived, the native people cut dugouts from the trunks of trees and used them to move between villages, as well as to hunt and fish. Canoes were the vehicle of necessity. In the summertime they paddled down to Lake Winnipeg to hunt buffalo, and in the winter they would come north to trap for beaver and other pelts. Like most native peoples, they rarely stayed in one place for very long, moving their villages and utilising what the land had to offer. All of it was done by canoe.

As we paddled, the river opened into a languid meander with barely a ripple on the surface; the atmosphere was very still, the sun high and scorching overhead. We saw an eagle skating close to the surface, where its shadow would be hidden by the trees. We saw fish jump and heard the noises of animals we couldn't see from deep within the forest. It was so peaceful, but only a little further on we came to the next set of rapids. When you see that white water up ahead, it's a dramatic shift of emotions: instead of easy paddling and the space for your mind to wander, your mouth is suddenly dry. This set was running much lower than Akeeko, however, and we glided down, the hull bucking slightly, with me dipping my paddle constantly while Cam used his to steer. Looking back, I saw Russ and Dave following our lead. Russ had this way of digging deep into the water with his paddle – there was something very earnest about it – and they hit the white water a little faster than we had. Everyone was safely through, though, and we paddled on. The water was flat once more and I thought about how a river like this must be full of ghosts, so many souls having passed this way: native people, French trappers, people like me. I was relaxed, thoroughly enjoying just being out here in this enormous silence.

But once again, the silence did not go on for ever. Up ahead was a beaver dam that forced the river into some pretty serious-looking water, and Cam directed us in close to the shore. When the boats were gathered, he and I paddled back to the middle so that he could scout out whether we could run the rapids, and if not, check out landing spots where we could portage the canoes. He thought they looked too steep to risk paddling with the boats loaded, so we would have to carry the gear around. He did suggest that once we'd done that, we could try just running the rapids for fun, with no equipment in the boat. I was up for that. I was having a great time, humming the tune to *Hawaii Five-O* and probably pissing Cam off a little by now.

With no beach to speak of, landing the canoe was easier said than done. The only suitable spot was a sloping slab of flat rock that we pulled alongside with difficulty. I had to hold the boat steady against the current while Cam stepped on to an underhang. Between us we swung the stern around and hauled the boat up the slab. Leaving the rest of us to sort the gear, he walked up to scout the rapids from the shore. They were serious: class three with a hole, a vortex of thrashing water at the bottom. That was where the currents mashed from opposing directions; if you were plonked in there, the pressure would keep you at the bottom, churn you up and eventually spit you out. Not a good place to be, and looking on, I doubted we'd be able to run them even with nothing in the boat. To be honest, though, I was a little blasé about it, more worried about the way my arse was itching. You see I'd been bitten on the bum by mozzies, and after a morning spent sitting in the boat, I was red raw.

Back from his recce, Cam pointed out the various rock pools that had been formed by millions of years of small stones being swirled around by the rushing water. Some of them were quite large and others tiny; some were kidney-shaped and others perfectly circular. One of them reminded me of my testicles: after a brush with cancer I've got only one; the other is an implant that is a little bigger than the real one. I made this point to anyone who was listening, and I think by now Cam was more than a little pissed off with me. As a punishment he told me he was going to show me how to solo portage. That's what Dave did earlier, swinging the heavy boat up and over his head.

Sixteen feet of unwieldy canoe weighs seventy-five pounds. They are designed for solo portage, though, with a central carrying yoke that sits on your shoulders. Tipping out the water, Cam told me to use my leg muscles rather than my back if I wanted to make it home. With the boat on its side and the hull against your legs, you lift and at the same time snap it over so that it's resting on your thighs. That was what Cam referred to as the intermediate position. The second move is to kick with your knee and roll the yoke across your shoulders while gripping the seat slat ahead of it. To my guide's consternation, I managed it without any trouble and carried it around the rapids, although there was no need to carry it at all, given that Cam had decided that we *could* risk the rapids with no gear in the canoes. I ended up having to carry it all back again, and I was beginning to wonder if this wasn't all part of some sadistic plan. I'd been watching the manic movement of water around the hole and all at once I forgot about my bites and the nerves began to kick in. Russ and I discussed the various permutations of leaving the boat unexpectedly and falling into the hole. We wondered whether you'd hit the bottom and get pinned there, or whether you'd pop out the other side. None of that made me feel any better, but I'm not one to turn my back on a challenge, and there was nothing for it but to have a go.

Thinking about it now, it was a bit like riding a motorbike on a race track. In discussion with Cam, I realised that there was only one line, and if you deviated from it, the chances were you'd capsize. My mouth was even drier now as I planned the route mentally from my vantage point on the shore. What would it look like head on? I wondered. Cam was confident. He reckoned that with the right kind of scouting from above, we ought to be able to pick our way through. I still wasn't sure, but this whole expedition was about testing ourselves and there was no way we were going to wimp out now.

The hole was obvious; the point where the currents literally reversed, with a wave coming back to smash into the one heading downstream. It was a mirror image of the tidal bore we'd experienced earlier in the trip, only it was static and fixed between this shoreline and the rocks on the other side. And that was weird too. I'd stare at the hole, then look at the rocks and I swear to God they were moving. I thought my eyes were giving up on me or something, but when I mentioned it, it was the same for all the guys.

Cam told me we needed to have the nose of the boat facing each obstacle, and I would control that by back-paddling while he steered us through. The nerves were beginning to turn into excitement now and I was ready to rock. Russ wasn't prepared for me to leave the safety of the shore just yet, though; I bet he was thinking of the rest of the show, and how he was going to swing it if Boorman died tragically there on the Bloodvein River. 'Cam,' he said. 'God forbid, but if Charley does flip out and get caught in that hole, what should he do?'

Cam just looked at him deadpan, eyes hidden behind his sunglasses, his helmet strapped low. 'There's nothing he can do,' he said. 'If that happens, you're finished. Game over.'

There was a moment's stunned silence before he smiled.

'No,' he added, 'if you do fall out, then take a breath before the water sucks you down. It's going to rag-doll you for a while but it will kick you out. The main thing to do is not panic, and each time you come up, grab a breath. Panic and you'll suck water – if that happens you *will* be finished, that's for sure.'

Paddling out, my heart was thumping and my hands were clammy. At the far bank we turned for the rapids to make sure we were coming at them from the right angle. It all hit us in a rush; from slack water we were suddenly into the first waves. The bows were pitching, water rushing over the side; we were hunkered left, avoiding the big rock, though the boat was almost on its side. I'd let go of the paddle with one hand and was gripping the gunwale; an absolute no-no in a canoe. Somehow we stayed upright, though Cam was yelling at me to let go. We were moving incredibly fast and now I was back-paddling, my gaze fixed on the rushing water that barrelled over the hole. It was on our left as it had to be, so that was a good thing, though only just, and all I could hear was the sound of millions of gallons of water churning over and over like some vast washing machine left on repeat spin. We brushed it at one point and I thought it would catch the bows, but we were off to the right and though the stern came round we made it unscathed.

'Yeah, baby!' The exhilaration was incredible. I was punching the air and yelling out at the top of my voice as we came about and paddled back to the others on the shore.

Cam had done a brilliant job, keeping calm and instructing me every step of the way. We had taken on a lot of water and it was sloshing around our knees, but he knew what he was doing and the scouting process had ensured we had a plan. (He did describe having me up front as some kind of beautiful chaos, though.) It was Russ and Dave's turn next. From where I was watching they seemed almost broadside, and for a moment I thought they were going to head right into the hole, but with the back-paddling and the way Dave was steering they kept their shape and just about shaved the lip.

Wow, what a morning. We'd gone from the serenity of flat water to dangerous, exhilarating rapids, and the day continued in that vein. That was the last really difficult set of rapids, mind you, and from then on we made it with our boats full of gear.

We camped for a second night with our gear strung on a line, and I bathed in the river and washed the surf out of my hair. Tents pitched properly this time, we ate dinner and I stood by the water and watched the sun go down.

*

Early the next morning we were on our way again. I was getting good at the rapids now, back-paddling and when we became stuck on rocks managing to get off again without grabbing the sides of the boat. There were a lot of rapids; every time another tributary entered the main flow, the junction was broken up by rocks. The last section before we reached the lodge where we were staying the night was pretty strenuous; a serious descent at a place called Four Battle Rapids. The still air from yesterday had been replaced by a stiff wind, and for most of the way it was right in our faces. By the time we steered the canoes to the jetty at Bloodvein River Lodge, I was feeling a little beaten up.

I slept really well – although water dominated my dreams – and the following morning we were back in the boats to travel a little further downstream to meet with the First Nations people. We were going to share a meal with a lady called Martina Fisher, and there was talk of us taking part in a sweat lodge ritual, part of the ancient purification traditions going back thousands of years. The construction of the sweat lodge was under way – a framework of reeds and tree branches that would be covered by lengths of tarpaulin, and next to it a great pile of stones. It was pitched in a grassy knoll close to Martina's clapboard house. We would have to get a serious fire going in order to heat the stones, but with my limbs a little weary, the idea of the sweat lodge was very appealing indeed.

The village was made up of single-storey wooden houses, all built fairly close to the water. Quite a few of the villagers were going to take part in the ceremony, and one young guy, wearing a baseball hat and wraparound sunglasses, was waiting for me to help him complete the lodge. He told me his name was Mari and he was the fire-keeper; his job was to pass what he called 'the grandfathers' into the lodge. These are the stones which symbolise the souls of tribal members who have passed on.

While the last preparations were being made, Cam took me across to meet Martina. She was a lovely woman, very welcoming, and sitting in her kitchen I asked her what the sweat lodge meant to her and to the community. Her answer surprised me. She told me that most people no longer practised any of the old ways. Prior to 1992 she hadn't either, but then she rediscovered her heritage and since then has taken part in the sun dance, been to various ceremonies and received teaching from the elders so she could perform some of the rites herself. She told me that not only did she have to learn the ancient rites, she had to earn the right to partake in them. Many of the old ways had been lost. It was hard to retain traditions when native language was banned and children were separated from their parents in order to assimilate them into European society, but there had been something of a resurgence of interest in the old ways recently, and Martina was hopeful about that.

Inside the sweat lodge, a person purifies their whole being – meaning the spiritual, the emotional and the mental as well as their actual body. In the old days, women did not go into the lodge; it was only for the men. Things were different now, though, because according to Martina it was the women who were teaching the men and bringing them back to the old ways.

I had no real idea of the old ways she was talking about, so I asked what I could expect. She told me that before we went in, we would purify ourselves with smoke from three of the four sacred medicines – sage, cedar and tobacco (the fourth is sweetgrass). Once we had been purified, we would enter the lodge on our hands and knees in order to humble ourselves. We would sit in a circle, with the strongest people to the west. There would be four doors, which we would open at intervals, starting in the east, then the south and west, and finally the north. The four doors represented the four directions, the four winds, the four races and the four stages of life: baby, child, adult and elder.

Martina went on to explain that the sweat lodge faces east in all Native American cultures, because east represents new life or new beginning; it's where the sun rises every morning. At the east door they pray for all children up to the age of twelve, even the ones yet to be born. At the south door, they think of the young people, the teenage years, when so many lives go wrong. At the west door, the prayers are for the adults – people like Martina herself and her friends. Finally, at the north door, they pray for the elders, the old people whose journey in this world is almost over.

She went on to talk about the spirits of their ancestors. Once a person has died, they normally go to the spirit world, but sometimes they wander. She said that spirits still need the help of the living, and in the sweat lodge they pray for them all.

Lunch was a wonderful meal of meat, vegetables and rice, along with home-made bread, and after we had finished we went outside. The lodge was almost prepared and the stones were heating. Martina carried a ceremonial drum she had spoken about earlier. She had a selection of chimes and rattles; she told me that they weren't just for this ceremony, but were also used in traditional medicine rites if a person was ill. She was convinced that the old ways were best, telling me how a few months previously she had been in a lot of abdominal pain. A visit to the hospital in Winnipeg confirmed that the problem was gallstones. That was all she needed to know. Back home, she went to see a medicine woman, who gave her some traditional remedies to dissolve the stones. She never took anything from the doctors at the hospital, had no treatment to remove the stones; just the herbs from the medicine woman, which got rid of the pain completely.

It was time for the ceremony. The only problem was the fact that we were not allowed to film inside. The sweat lodge is sacred, and entry is permitted only to those participating in the ritual. Martina said that we would be calling up the spirits of their ancestors, who would not want their images to show up in the film. Some things are just meant to be private, I suppose, so that was the way it would be.

Martina heated a clump of sage over some hot coals that she plucked straight from the fire, and we palmed the smoke over our faces. I took it very seriously, having a word with my sister Telsche as I performed the rite. Then I walked in a circle around the fire pit, clockwise as was the custom. Taking a garden fork, Cam shifted ten heated stones into the lodge, and with Nat the last to purify himself, we closed the eastern door.

It was a real experience. Martina spoke about the varying stages of life while we sat there in a circle, cross-legged with sweat pouring off our bodies. It was pitch black, the only light the glow from the red-hot rocks. I stared at those rocks almost all the time we were in there, and at one point I could make out the most beautiful face. I felt completely relaxed, listening to Martina's voice, the beat of the drum. She broke the ceremony up into several sessions, and as each door was opened we took a moment to catch some fresh air. It was just as well, because it was incredibly hot in there and to remain inside without a break would've been unbearable. I really got involved, thinking about my children, my family and friends, people I've lost; at times it was very emotional.

Afterwards I sat outside with one of the local guys, Norman, who had only recently revisited his traditional heritage. He told me that when their traditions were forcibly taken away from them, each successive generation of elders spoke about how they would return, and little by little they had. What struck me was that when we were remembering the children, teenagers, adults and elders, our thoughts weren't confined just to those in the community. There was, as Norman put it, no discrimination; the ceremony had been held for every member of every race, young and old, right across the world. Maybe that's something the government and the churches in the nineteenth century didn't appreciate.

7

Police Academy

After the sweat lodge I felt great – refreshed, really at peace with myself, and that's not something that happens very often. Anyone who's read my previous books will know how I worry, get the heebie-jeebies about stuff when probably there's no need. But after that experience in the lodge, I really was pretty chilled out.

The following morning I woke up thinking about the river trip – the rush of adrenalin as we hit the water for the first time in those canoes; how to begin with, it was all a bit tough because we didn't really know what we were doing and we'd everything to learn. It's the second day when you start to relax; you know, get over the fact that you have no phone signal, that kind of thing. Pretty soon you don't want a phone signal; pretty soon you begin to appreciate why people come here to this wilderness and just lose themselves for a few weeks at a time. It's therapeutic, an escape from the everyday stuff you have to deal with, the pressures you put on yourself. You're paddling, dealing with the river, and that takes all your concentration. Your day is broken into pieces and it's all you think about: getting up and paddling, making for the shore, paddling again. After only a couple of days I was totally into it, and I suppose the longer you're out here, the more that rhythm is established.

This morning the plan was to paddle the last stretch from the Bloodvein River Lodge to the point where the MV *Edgar Wood* ferry runs across Lake Winnipeg to the western shore. It was a short crossing, and when we landed, Cam's base crew were there to greet us with a van and trailer for the canoes. They drove us the three or so hours back to Winnipeg, where we spent another night at the Fort Garry Hotel, although this time I steered clear of the haunted room.

After our few days in the wilderness, it was back on the bikes to our next stop: Regina, Saskatchewan, three hundred and fifty miles west of Winnipeg. We were planning to hook up with the Royal Canadian Mounted Police and I was going to see what it would be like to be a cadet. It was a little daunting; the Mounties are iconic: think of Canada and you think of that red jacket and flat-brimmed Stetson.

Driving into Regina, we passed branches of McDonald's and Taco Bell – it seemed to me that the further west we travelled, the more like America the cityscapes were becoming. I suppose it was bound to be that way; the States was just south of here and there are a lot of similarities anyway. Having said that, when you hit the outskirts of most British cities these days, it's KFC and Burger King that greet you.

But we weren't in Britain; we were crossing the second largest country in the world and the diversity so far had been incredible. We'd seen the Atlantic coastline; we'd seen lakes and rivers and forests; and now the land was pancake flat as far as the eye could see. Not only was Manitoba flat, it was very, very hot. As we drove into town, the temperature was thirty-three degrees Celsius and I was in leather jacket, jeans and helmet. Stopping at a set of lights, Canadian White Van Man pulled up alongside and yelled across to me: 'Hey, Charley, what're you doing here?' The second person to recognise me! 'Man, I love your shows, dude. This is awesome.'

I told him that I was heading for training with the Mounties, and he wished me luck. It's great that people do that: just show up and chat away as if you're an old friend. I was reminded of heading off on *Long Way Round* all those years ago with Ewan, when a similar guy in a white van in London wished us all the luck in the world.

Riding along, I kept thinking about the movie *Police Academy* and what might lie in store for me. The Mounties are tough and I knew their training was second to none; they're renowned for training police forces from all over the world. Hopefully they wouldn't run me too ragged. I mean, I'm forty-five now and a little portly. I'm bike-fit – I'm always bike-fit – but I wasn't sure I was quite Mountie-fit, if you see what I mean.

Even though we got lost on the way (it was bound to happen at some point, I suppose), we eventually found the place. It was a pretty splendid-looking red-brick building set back from the road in lush-looking lawns. Parking the BMW outside the front doors, I climbed off, stripped off my helmet and wiped the sweat from my brow. Russ went in, but a few minutes later came out again to tell us that this was the wrong place. This was their headquarters; we wanted the training centre. Apparently the people he'd spoken to inside hadn't been the most helpful – they didn't actually give us the address of where we had to go; they just told us to head back to the lights and turn left. Before we did that, we took a breather; three bikes and four sweat-soaked travellers: we were all a little bushed after the heat of this morning and those last few days in the canoe.

Just as our first impressions of the Mounties looked to be a little tainted, a cop in a marked white pickup swung by and told us he'd take us to the training centre. Saddled up, we followed him down the street and made the turn suggested to Russ. I thanked the cop and he told me that I'd better expect boot camp, because that's what this place was. That made me nervous, but I kept telling myself it couldn't be that bad, and it was only a day after all.

We had to stop at some very tall gates in a very tall fence, ten feet at least, with barbed wire encircling the top. This was the real deal, and I admit my stomach was churning. Checked through, we rode round to where they'd asked us to park the bikes. Dan was waiting for us; he was a corporal from the communications section, wearing a blue uniform and a cap with a yellow band. A cheery chappie, he told us that his job was to meet and greet people like us and delegates from other police forces, and teach them how the RCMP did the things it did. He showed us into a red-brick building, 'Centralized Training', where we would check in, then took me down to get kitted out in shorts and socks, all ready for my training day tomorrow. Gulp! Now the nerves were really kicking in.

On the way down to the stores, we talked a little about the history of the RCMP and Dan explained about the horses, the mounted bit of the mounted police. Apparently they were actually phased out between the mid sixties and early seventies, although there was still an equine training centre in Ottawa. They were mostly used for ceremonial purposes these days, rather than actual police work.

We were now in C Block; built in 1953, it's the original leathercraft shop where the famous riding boots the Mounties wear are made. Inside, the signs were both in French and English. Dan led me down to meet Sean, the stores guy, who said he had some goodies lined up for me. Bringing out a blue kitbag, he revealed a white RCMP cadet T-shirt with my name emblazoned across it.

'Ah,' I said. 'You've been expecting me, haven't you?'

'Oh yeah, that we have.'

He gave me a red rubber gun, the size and shape of an automatic, to fit the holster he would also be issuing. Then he kitted me out with trousers that were too long but would be taken up, and a pair of white RCMP socks, and told me I'd be getting some body armour just like any other cadet. I was trying to take it in – all this for only one day. As I was thinking about what they might have lined up for me, I glimpsed the iconic red jackets hanging on a rack. Now if I could just get one of those . . .

With the amount of stuff Sean was piling on to the counter, I really was beginning to feel nervous, and I asked him if that was normal. Did all 'newbies', as he called them, feel this way?

'All of them,' he said. 'They sit up front there at the

counter and it's like a bunch of rabbits caught in the headlights, really. Relax, Charley. Trust me, buddy, you're not alone.'

Soon we got on to the fun stuff: the gear belt where the holster would fit, the radio, the mace spray and whatever else they carried. Then it was the cap, blue with a yellow band – similar to Dan's. That was all very well, but what about the Stetson? The iconic hat of the Mountie? Sean found one for me to try on and told me that the cadets get issued with them pretty much as soon as they arrive, but they have to earn the right to wear them and that takes six long months. As I tried it on over my RCMP regulation-length hair (as if), Dan told me to tilt it slightly to the right, as that was my saluting hand. Jaunty, then. I could be jaunty for sure.

Opening another box, Sean brought out the riding boots – knee-length, lace-up and a sort of chocolate brown. This was the raw state, before they were brushed and polished to the point where you could see your face in them. These days the boots were worn mostly at functions and ceremonies, but Sean did say that the motorcycle units wore them every day, along with the big jodhpur-type pants that look so cool. When he added that they rode bespoke Harley-Davidsons, I decided that when my turn came to 'graduate', I would opt for the bike division right away.

Next he showed me the winter hat; a fur cap that people

think is beaver but is actually made from muskrat. The body armour was much lighter than the stuff I'd been issued when I flew into Afghanistan to meet the troops. That had ceramic plates in it, and as we flew into Kandahar, we were told to sit on the armour because the Taliban liked to shoot at the belly of the plane. No wonder this was lighter, though; the bulletproof panels weren't in it yet. Sean issued those separately and showed me how to put the whole thing together – this is the most important piece of kit each cadet is given. The armour is Kevlar and you think it's solid, but it's not. Kevlar is cloth, and there are twenty-one layers in each panel. Sean showed me a suit that had been marked in three places, the result of being hit by 9mm rounds fired from three metres away. Only the first layer of Kevlar had been penetrated; the wearer might've been bruised but they didn't die. So they were going to shoot at me, were they? Jesus, Russ: what are you doing to me, buddy?

The crime rate in Canada is nothing compared to America; the only really bad places are a handful of small towns in northern British Columbia. The average murder rate in the capital, Ottawa, for example, is three homicides a year. That's not very many, nowhere near London, where last year 125 people were murdered. Even so, Sean reiterated that the body armour is the most important piece of kit the cadets are issued, and we packed it into the bag. He almost forgot the

judogi – the white suit martial arts experts wear; he told me
I was definitely going to need that.

Kitted out in my summer shirt and cadet epaulettes, I
really was beginning to feel like a new, very raw recruit. Next
we went to the tailor's shop, where my trousers had already
been sent to be altered. At the counter I bumped into another
brand-new cadet. He was about thirty feet tall and he wasn't
even wearing the boots. He told me he had had his first drill
yesterday and it was hardcore.

'So how long have you got here?' I asked him.

'Only another five months, three weeks and two days, but
hey, who's counting?'

He was so tall – six feet ten, or 208 centimetres, whichever
you prefer – he'd had to have extra-long shirts specially
made. A little taller than me, then. I'd probably see him
around; he was the tallest cadet they'd had in years and I was
unlikely to miss him, that's for sure. When he was gone, I
asked the woman behind the counter if she knew anything
about my trousers; with nineteen seamstresses working back
there, she just handed them to me already done.

Dan told me that at 0600 tomorrow morning I had to be
dressed correctly in shirt, pants, belt and cap – which you put
on by holding the crown, by the way, never the brim,
otherwise it would be perpetually smothered in fingerprints
and you'd be hauled over the coals for that. Meeting up with

the rest of Troop 2, I would proceed to morning parade. The drill staff would be there to inspect me and make sure I was wearing the uniform properly.

Further down the concourse we saw Troop 2 being drilled, kitted out in shirts, trousers and body armour with their blue kitbags slung over their shoulders and the dummy guns in their holsters. A sergeant-major-type guy was yelling at them, although it turned out he was just another cadet. I watched from a safe distance, taking shade under a tree; tomorrow and tomorrow and tomorrow, as my dad used to say when he was quoting Shakespeare. They came marching down the block like a well-oiled machine. I just knew I was going to let them down.

They halted right where we were filming, wheeled to the left then broke off. The guy drilling them was what they call a 'right marker', someone facilitating their movements around the camp. He told me that although the day was officially over, that evening some of them had firearms training, while others were doing patrol drives, and they had to get all their paperwork squared away.

They gave me cell number D153 for the night. Not a cell actually, but a spacious room with its own bathroom and a comfortable bed; given how hot it was outside, it was also reasonably cool. Dan told me that I was privileged: if I was a regular cadet, I'd be in one of thirty-two beds in one long dormitory for the next six months of my life. I got some sleep, although not much, and at 0600, as instructed, I hit the parade ground with the rest of Troop 2. When I say 0600, I was perhaps a fraction late ... As the last one there, I had to walk past every other eagle-eyed recruit to find my place. Of course, they stuck me in the front row. I made my introductions and promised them I would try not to let them down, but already it was looking like a complete disaster. I had some buttons done up in the wrong places and others undone in the wrong places. I was wearing my dummy gun, which apparently I shouldn't be. We hadn't even started yet.

I had no idea what to expect. I knew nothing about anything and Dan suggested to the other cadets that they ought to take advantage of that, because I would be taking the brunt of everything that morning. I even got the stand to attention all wrong: right foot instead of left. 'I'm dyslexic,' I said. 'I get muddled.' My cap wasn't on straight and I was considerably chubbier than the other recruits. My hair was long, my expression nowhere near as serious as it should be.

The cadet next to me told me that after parade and before breakfast they had to clean up their dormitory, something I'd be spared at least. Last night he had got to bed at about twelve after sorting his files, polishing his boots and ironing his shirt for this morning. The files were reports written on various scenarios they had practised, as if they had been at a crime scene or an accident and were writing up the appropriate paperwork. The actual work day starts at eight, but they're up at five to get ready for parade, and the evenings are spent doing stuff like the patrol drives I mentioned. It's a massive commitment but they all seem to love it – working as a team, determined that every member of the troop will graduate with flying colours.

For the next ten minutes I experienced a little of what they would go through for the last four months of their training: I was shouted at while standing at ease, trying to stand to attention, and marching in lines of four, in step, arms swinging back and forth in unison. Finally it was time for inspection. This big guy walked over, wearing knee-length boots with studs in the leather soles that made them crackle over the tarmac. Swagger stick under his arm, he took one look at me before reminding me that Elvis was dead and my sideburns were too long, and pointing out that my shirt was wrinkled, there was no shine on my shoes and my hat was crooked.

'Frankly, Boorman,' he said, 'you look like you survived a train wreck.' He walked round behind me. 'Where did you find that shirt? It looks like a road map it's got so many wrinkles. You need to see the barber, son – you look like a bear.'

Parade over, mercifully, I had to report for my 'pairs' – an exercise you have to complete in four minutes or you're asked to leave. Basically it's an assault course designed to simulate some of the obstacles you might encounter on the beat. It occurred to me then that if I failed, they'd probably send me home early, which might not be a bad thing.

If my shirt didn't fit properly, then the T-shirt certainly didn't. They'd given me an XL and it reached almost to my knees. Of course I'd forgotten something – I always do, and this time it was my socks. Already half into my kit, I had to get back into full uniform, including my hat – a cadet cannot go anywhere on camp without being dressed properly – and run back to try and locate the missing pair of RCMP-issue socks, while the rest of the troop were getting ready to warm up.

So I jogged back to my room, working up a sweat I should have been saving for later. Mungo commented that I was taking it very seriously, but everyone around me was fully committed and I would feel terrible if I was just taking the piss. I had to look hard for the socks; they were nowhere to be seen. I'm not the tidiest person, but it was a small room – they had to be somewhere! Finally I found them, stuffed, for some reason, down the back of my bed. I was beginning to suspect sabotage. Where was Russ, anyway?

Stupid as it might sound, I suddenly felt homesick. I'd convinced myself I was going to let the side down, make a fool of myself, and all I wanted to do was go home. I mean, only an idiot forgets his socks. What was I thinking?

In the gym and finally dressed correctly for the pairs run, I spoke to a cadet who was originally from England. He'd been in Canada thirteen years, had married a French Canadian, and told me he'd joined up because it was every young Canadian boy's dream to become a Mountie. He was only a week into his training, but along with the rest of the cadets – bar me, obviously – he was enjoying every second.

They checked my blood pressure and told me I was good to go. Pity. I warmed up with a cadet who had just completed the course in two minutes and fifty-five seconds. That was pretty good, given that the record was two seventeen. I had to do it in less than four minutes and I was determined not to let anybody down.

The course was a five-lap run around a series of cones, up and down some steps, and over small jumps and a vault where you hit the ground on either your back or your front, depending on which lap you were on. I tried to set a pace I was comfortable with and I had the encouragement of my troop behind me. It was tough: five consistent laps then on to a machine where you push your weight against pressured bars as if you're wrestling with a suspect. You wheel the machine from side to side, then it's on your back and up again, on to your stomach, up again, and this time instead of pushing the weights you're pulling them. When I was finished, my hands were on my knees as I waited for the time with bated breath. Three minutes and fifty-four seconds – that gave me a full six seconds to spare. I had done it!

Back in uniform, I was introduced to three instructors: Craig, who was dressed in the kind of dark-coloured fatigues SWAT guys wear, Paul and Ian. They told me to change into the judo pants and T-shirt; then, joining the rest of Troop 2, we strapped on our gun belts and made our way to another gym with padded walls and floor, where we all started running around. I had no idea what was going on. I was either being inducted into a mental asylum or was about to take part in some kind of self-defence class, but it was hard to tell. Ian had us working on loosening exercises for our hips, shoulders and arms. Rolling my hips from side to side, I commented to Mungo that it was at times like this that I missed my wife. No time for the joke to register, though, because now we were throwing ourselves flat on the floor. It felt like being in playschool, only much sweatier. I was just following what the others did and it took a moment for me to realise that we were practising falls, rolling with a throw or a punch, taking a suspect down with us. It went on and on and on. Finally we started working with a partner, in my case a very fit-looking guy with a shaved head who proceeded to toss me around like a rag doll.

When we'd finished in the padded room, I crawled back into my uniform for another parade. Then I was off to meet Dion, a corporal who was to be my driving instructor. At last some respite, some action other than the physical stuff that I'd just about had enough of. When Dion mentioned the words 'collision avoidance track' I brightened considerably.

The car was a Ford Crown Victoria, which is standard police issue in North America. As we made our way over to the track, Dion told me that he'd graduated twenty years before but had come back to teach the new cadets how to drive a police car properly. He showed me how to drive at speed towards a number of cones and swerve to avoid them safely. Only he stalled the engine. Well, maybe he didn't. We came to a sudden stop because I hadn't realised that there were brakes on my side too; I had my foot planted on the pedal.

A few more runs – with me off the brake this time – and then it was my turn. This was much more like it: behind the wheel of a police car and driving hard. Anything with an engine (especially an up-rated V8 like this) and I am in my element. With no cones disturbed on my first go, Dion told me I was ready to attempt a J-turn – that's driving backwards, swinging around to face the other way and driving off again in one smooth motion. He did it first – wheels screeching, we raced backwards, then he spun the car and before I knew it we were facing the other way and speeding off once more. When my turn came, I have to say it was as smooth as a knife through hot butter. Even Dion was impressed. The only thing was, I'd swung to the left instead of the right, which wasn't so safe given that in Canada they drive on the right-hand side of the road.

From the track, we moved to the underground shooting range and the more serious side of police work. Down there with Troop 2 all letting rip with 9mm automatics, the noise was pretty loud. They were firing at targets fifty metres away, round after round after round. It's all about speed, safety and accuracy, and these guys were very good. One cadet shooting right in front of me had all his rounds in a group no more than a few inches apart.

When it was time for my turn, they told I wasn't going to shoot at targets. Not just yet anyway. No, what they had in mind for me was much more realistic. My instructor took me to another room and I was given an automatic to replace the rubber gun in my holster. I was about to take part in a movie – an interactive scenario that would be screened on to the wall in front of me. I'd been called to a building where people with guns were shooting each other and I had to determine who was a threat and who was not. I had plenty of questions for my instructor: should I have my gun holstered or drawn? What could I expect?

'Well,' he said carefully, 'you're answering a call where people are shooting each other inside a building.'

That was the point, of course: you never know what to expect – every call a Mountie receives is different and you can assume nothing. Pistol drawn, I was in a building where an alarm was sounding, following another cop. I could see somebody lying motionless on the floor and ahead of me the cop was unloading his weapon into one of the rooms.

Then it was my turn: a bad guy with a handgun levelled at me. 'Get on the ground!' I yelled. 'Get on the ground!' He didn't move, so I had no choice. I tried to shoot him but my gun jammed and the bastard killed me.

After my instructors checked my gun, we did the same thing in another building. This time there was a wounded man lying on the floor of a corridor calling for help. Ignoring him, I moved on as a screaming woman came rushing out of a room at the far end. Inside I found a man with a gun pointed at another guy who was on his knees in front of him, while a woman in the corner was screaming at the top of her voice.

'Police officer!' I yelled. 'Put your gun down. Put your gun down now.' He wasn't listening. He shot the guy on his knees and I had no choice but to pop him.

Afterwards I asked the instructor if I'd been too slow to react, but he pointed out that I didn't know if the man was going to shoot. He'd been waving the gun at both the man in front of him and the woman in the corner and at some point a judgement had to be made. If I was a real cop, that judgement would be based on my experience, training and instinct. Maybe I made it too late, I don't know. But I had no choice but to bring him down. 'Ultimately,' the instructor said, 'you have to be able to explain why you made the decision you did.'

Personally I'm not a fan of firearms and I'm grateful that our police force doesn't carry guns on an everyday basis. But as my instructor pointed out, it's all about the culture of a country, and although police officers in Canada carry guns, it's a vastly different culture to the United States, with a fraction of the population and a much lower crime rate. Everyone has a view, of course, and back home it's always an ongoing discussion. I know plenty of people who believe our police officers should be routinely armed; I'm just not one of them. It was great to do the simulation, though, and I can see how beneficial it would be for the cadets. I'd been edgy, jerky in my movements, but the instructor pointed out that the more familiar you are with your side arm, the more relaxed you'll be, and when you're relaxed you think more clearly.

I was impressed, not just with the whole Mountie training, but with myself. All in all, this day as an RCMP cadet had not gone badly at all. It's not something I think I'd want to do for a living – the whole thing is a little too regimented for someone like me – but it was great fun and a privilege to have been allowed to go through it. I knew that every member of Troop 2 was going to graduate, no problem.

The next day was 1 July, Canada Day, which commemorates confederation in 1867, something we knew all about from our time on Prince Edward Island. We were still in Regina and there was to be a big celebration with a massive fireworks display, so we thought it would be great to hang around and see what went on.

Downtown at the Saskatchewan Legislative Building, we wandered among the crowds. Wandering was all I could manage – after my day with the Mounties, I was aching from the waist down. Across the park from the legislature there was a fair going on with music playing, and we gathered over there. Russ was being nibbled by mosquitoes and his mind was on finding somewhere that sold bug spray, but when that wasn't forthcoming he opted for candyfloss instead. There was this one fantastic truck with a smokehouse for ribs and chicken actually built into the trailer. I spoke to the owner's son and he told me that they had a restaurant in the city and this was how they serviced outdoor events. The family were Americans from Oklahoma; this guy's father had been in the military originally, based in Canada, and when he left, he opened the restaurant and stayed.

We were walking along by the lake, and after a while I sat down on a rug next to a middle-aged lady and asked her what Canada Day meant to her. She thought about it for a moment before she answered. She told me that apart from it being a holiday, her daughter, who worked as a teacher in Egypt, always came home for Canada Day. Her plane was landing about now and her dad was picking her up and bringing her to the lake for the fireworks. The woman was interesting to chat to, describing herself as a flag-waver in a way that lots of Canadians don't. She said that the Americans were flag-wavers but that most Canadians were a bit reticent about being too overtly patriotic – I put it down to the British influence, a stiff upper lip and all that. Her only gripe about this Canada Day was that given that Regina was the Queen's city, she felt that Wills and Kate, who were on a tour of the country, should be here rather than in Ottawa. She admitted to being a bit of a royal fanatic and was delighted that Canada's younger generation seemed to have taken the royal couple to their hearts.

I was so pleased to have been there for Canada Day. In every city across the country Canadians were celebrating the anniversary of confederation. We don't have anything like that at home; in England, nobody bothers much with St George's Day – if anything, St Patrick's Day takes precedence. As the fireworks began, I decided that we ought to adopt the sentiment and have a Britain Day maybe. Why not?

8
Parallel Lines

I've hung around the film business most of my life, and I can tell you that if you talk to any actor, they'll confess that the one genre they all want to be in is a Western. I'm no different. I'd love to be in a Western, and I know Ewan would too. Perhaps we could do one together, remake *Butch Cassidy* or something. Right then, though, the chance of me getting a call from the Coen brothers seemed slim, so I decided to settle for the real thing and the Circle Y ranch in the Badlands of the Big Muddy in southern Saskatchewan.

I slid my way on the bike around a gravel road that twisted through low-lying hills that were green and dusty. It was another baking day, the sky overhead clear and blue, and we arrived at the clutch of buildings that make up the

Circle Y in the heat of the midday sun. Sitting on the porch in his hickory rocker was the owner, Michael Burgess. We were in a remote spot, very isolated, and Michael told me that in the winter they sometimes had people walk down to the yard after getting stuck in the snow on the hill. As he put it, theirs were the only yard lights for miles in any direction.

Much of the twenty thousand acres Michael ranched was rugged grazing land that he rented from the government in thirty-three-year blocks. Originally it was his grandfather who came out here; an entrepreneur with various businesses in southern Ontario, he'd had a yearning to ranch, and the family had now been here for seventy-four years. When I made the mistake of asking Michael how he farmed, he put me straight right away.

'We ranch,' he said. 'We don't farm. Farming generally means cultivating the land. The only crop we grow is hay, permanent cover that we cut every year. Basically we're a cow-calf ranch, Charley: that means we run cows and raise calves to sell either to dairy farms or feed lots.'

He told me it was a hard business that had hit a really low point with the BSE crisis in 2003. Things were finally getting better now, though, with the export markets opening up again.

'Having said that,' he added, 'input costs keep going up,

with fuel and whatnot, so I don't know if we're getting any farther ahead. We just feel better about it, I guess.'

I'd been studying the map before we got here and worked out that this ranch ran almost right down to the American border. When you look at the map you can't help but notice how the border is very squiggly back east but then becomes this long, straight line once you get on to the plains. I asked Michael why that was, and he told me that back in the days of the first settlers, the Americans were lobbying hard to take more of western Canada and the Canadians were fighting hard to keep it. In the end, the politicians settled matters by agreeing that the 49th Parallel should form the border in this area. As with many borders, however, the people living on either side are pretty similar, with most of them making their living from the land. Tammy, Michael's wife, was American. He told me how he and his two neighbours decided to find themselves American wives, so they headed across the border. In Tammy's case, although she changed country, she only moved four miles house to house when she married him.

In the past, the border area wasn't as heavily patrolled as it is now. When cattle crossed over, as they were wont to do, there was no problem with the authorities in Montana when Michael and his hands went to get them back. That all changed after 9/11. Since then the US Department of

Homeland Security has tightened things up considerably. Now, they patrol in SUVs and on quads, and they also fly both manned and unmanned aircraft over the area.

We talked about the old days – Prohibition, when the rum runners would shift white lightning back and forth to speakeasies and blind pigs in the US. Given that this was pretty rough country, however, there wasn't that much smuggling going on up here. Michael made the point that the Badlands wasn't the easiest place to run illicit booze, but it did make a great hideout for outlaws at the turn of the twentieth century. Train robbers and bank robbers, horse thieves from the US, they all would come up from what back then was Valley County, Montana, to hide out in the Big Muddy Badlands of Saskatchewan. Eventually it was such a problem that the North-West Mounted Police (as they were then) dispatched a couple of men from their post at Wood Mountain, but even that didn't help much, as I would find out later.

The area was also rife with horse rustling. Michael told us about a horse thief named Kid Trailer. Kid Trailer was a young guy who played the fiddle and was a favourite at dances on both sides of the border. Apparently he was playing one night in Antelope, Montana, when the sheriff recognised him and arrested him. He tied the kid up and was going to take him home to Culbertson, but the dance-goers broke him out so he could finish playing.

I was keen to see if Michael could get us down to the border. From the beginning of this expedition we had wanted to push the boundaries of Canada, and we'd already done that on the east coast.

I'd ridden here on the BMW, of course, but as soon as I saw Lane's truck, I fell hopelessly in love with it. Lane is Michael's son, who recently bought his own ranch that butts right against the border. He had this really cool 1984 Dodge Prospector pickup, which was on its third engine and gearbox; it had a short bed, which made it unstable, as did the height it had been jacked up to. He told me it wasn't safe to drive. In fact, that's an understatement; the word he actually used was 'insane'. It sits up too high, rolls easily and therefore doesn't corner very well – and this was rough and rugged country. Nothing on the truck was original. Lane had replaced the half-ton chassis with one from a one-ton truck instead; inside the cab, the taped-up bench seat was from an earlier model. He told me that most of the parts in the vehicle were 'after market'.

'That there used to be shiny,' he said, pointing to the steering rack as we lifted the bonnet. 'The pump fell off the other day. I'd never even touched it but it fell off anyway. I guess over time most of what you see has fallen off. Got it fixed back, though, and it only squeaks a little.'

He let me drive, and it was fantastic; massive knobbly

tyres and the paintwork all covered in dust. Michael came with me and I took the opportunity to ask him more about the area. He told me that the yard at their ranch sits right across what was the old Willow Bunch Trail, along which Jean-Louis Légaré, the trading-post operator from Willow Bunch, had escorted Sitting Bull and his people back to the US to surrender to the army in the late 1800s.

I loved driving that truck; of all the vehicles I've ever driven, it ranks way up there with the best of them. It felt like it was part of Canada, part of the American continent, part of the west, I suppose. I drove with the window rolled down and my elbow on the sill. The bumps in the road, the rock-hard suspension, the play in the steering – this was what driving in North America is all about. The experience had made me a little emotional. I told Mungo that it had been the highlight of my whole Canada trip. Never mind canoeing or climbing or making nails with the Vikings; it was all about this truck.

We reached a gate with a signpost for the Giles Ranch. A sign outside told us that 'Trespassers will be given a fair trial then hung'. Just to make it doubly clear for those who didn't understand English, there was a picture of a neatly tied noose draped over a tree branch. We really were deep in the Great Plains here and it's hard to get across just how huge the distances are. The American side is pretty desolate and the Canadian side is nowhere near as densely populated – the nearest town is Big Beaver, where fresh fruit and vegetables are delivered to the store every Thursday. Michael and Tammy try to get to town once a week to pick up groceries and the mail, and when their children were still at school, they had to travel fifty miles there and back on the bus.

We drove a little further, through a collection of small hills and white-faced bluffs that personified the Badlands. It was dusty; there hadn't been much rain here lately. Finally we arrived. I could see the pyramid-shaped hill named Peak Butte that marked the border. There was a pole on top, and normally a flag would be flying, but for some reason nobody had erected one this year. This side of the hill was Saskatchewan and the far side Montana; we really were at the extreme frontier.

The whole area is littered with caves; this was the sort of place where the train robbers of old would have holed up. It was a notorious hideout of the Wild Bunch, a loose configuration of bandits who congregated here in the late 1800s. With the price of beef crashing and ranches going broke as far south as Texas, unemployed cowboys migrated up here and fell into collective thievery. The caves were named after Sam Kelly, who ran the Nelson-Jones gang; a wooden sign marks the entrance to what was originally an old wolf den that Kelly and his men had enlarged.

This was the northernmost point in the Outlaw Trail, a

series of intersecting routes created by Butch Cassidy that allowed him to make his escape after robbing the Union Pacific Railroad time and again. By the time he was finished, Cassidy had a notorious secret path that ran all the way from Canada to Mexico, with way stations (usually friendly ranches) every fifteen miles. Outlaws could hold up a train or rob a bank, then use the trail to make their way north or south to safety, and the authorities couldn't get close.

Not far from the old wolf den was a larger cave dug from the hills that could house a dozen horses. Michael told me about Dutch Henry, probably the most successful horse thief of all time. He would steal herds from ranchers in Montana, drive them to Canada and sell them, then steal them back and drive them south to Wyoming or Deadwood in Dakota territory, where he would sell them again.

The Circle Y is in Huntley Coulee, named after Jasper Huntley, a rancher from the old days who was a friend of the outlaws. He'd use his running iron to change the brand on horses stolen in America. When the Mounted Police dispatched those two guys from Wood Mountain to patrol the Big Muddy, they ended up staying with Huntley and consequently didn't have much success in catching anybody. Whatever they told him or he overheard, he'd pass to the outlaws so they could evade capture.

On the other side of the valley from the Burgess place is

Carlisle Coulee, named after Frank Carlisle, a Mountie who, according to Michael, 'went bad' and hooked up with a bunch of train robbers. One day he got drunk and was sleeping it off on the Marshall Ranch when he was supposed to be in Montana blowing up a bridge to stop a train. Because of that there was no robbery, and two members of the Wild Bunch rode to the Marshall place, grabbed Frank and took him to Carlisle Coulee, where they shot him dead.

There's another coulee further north known as Roan Mare; it was named after a horse that would swim the treacherous Big Muddy Lake without hesitation. When they became aware of that phenomenon, the outlaws would bring up stolen horses and get the mare to lead them across the lake. That gave them an advantage over the Mounties who were chasing them, because they would have to ride around the lake, by which time the outlaws were long gone. The bed of the lake is alkaline and therefore soft, and in the shallows it can suck you down. Somehow the roan mare sensed that and knew how to pick her way across.

Thinking about it, those outlaws were pretty smart guys. Taking the lead from Butch Cassidy, they devised routes and trails and cultivated friendships with ranchers to make sure they always had the drop on the lawmen who were pursuing them.

I got to drive the Dodge up on to the hill overlooking

Montana. A creek ran between the hills and it was easy to see how a whole gaggle of outlaws could disappear in a place like this. It was staggeringly beautiful: copses of trees and the creek meandering below me and nothing on the horizon but rolling hills and that big sky they talk about in Montana. Standing high on a rock, I was on the southern frontier of Canada. We'd started on the easternmost lip and now we were in the south, and just a stone's throw away from America.

Leaving the caves, we drove along a narrow strip of empty road to the border crossing that lies between Big Beaver, Saskatchewan, and White Tail, Montana. The Canadian post had been closed some time ago, and stopping the truck, I walked around the barrier that marks the end of Canada. Now I was in no-man's-land, and ahead of me was US Border Station 1. There the colour of the road changed from gritty white to a pinkish colour marked with yellow lines.

The US border agent walked up to see us; he knew Michael and his wife Tammy, but I suppose he wondered what I was doing prancing up and down while Mungo recorded my every move with the camera. He was a nice guy named Carl, and he spoke to us about how things were changing in Canada. With the drug wars going on in Mexico, the border agents down there were all over it, which meant that some of the cartels were shipping drugs up the coast and bringing them into the States from Canada. On top of that there was the problem of terrorists, although he figured there were probably enough of those already in America to do all the damage they wanted.

I stared out across the border. The land of opportunity was just a few short steps away. But that was for another time and another adventure. I jumped back into the Dodge, ready for my next stop: Alberta.

9

Old King Coal

Alberta sits directly to the west of Saskatchewan and is the fourth largest of the ten provinces at over 600,000 square kilometres. When you consider that the entire United Kingdom is only 240,000 square kilometres, that's still pretty huge! It is very much cowboy country, still, famous for the largest rodeo in the world, the Calgary Stampede, and we were hoping to catch that while we were there. But before we even reached Calgary, we stopped for fuel in the small town of Maple Creek, still in Saskatchewan, and discovered another rodeo. Not quite the Stampede, but it was taking place today and we had to check it out. Yesterday in the Badlands had been all about the old-time cowboys; now we had a chance to see the modern-day version displaying their skills in the arena.

We had no idea what to expect when we arrived at the rodeo grounds. I asked around and was told that this was an annual event where local ranch hands had the chance to show their skills at roping and branding, penning cattle and riding a saddle bronc. There's a part of every guy that wants to be a cowboy, and I really wanted to get involved. The organisers told us that a saddle bronc – an unbroken horse bred to buck – was too dangerous.

They would let me have a go on a cow. So I'd be riding a steer then, like the children, when I'd been imagining climbing the rail like Steve McQueen in *Junior Bonner*: it would be like the ice hockey all over again. Oh well, at least there was less risk of broken bones. Wandering over to the main arena, we watched a few contestants putting some horses through their paces. We took a seat up in the bleachers and I looked out beyond the metal fences – there was nothing but the road between us and the horizon far, far in the distance. It's flat around Maple Creek, so flat there doesn't really seem to be much of a horizon at all. I found that I was missing the cliffs of the Big Muddy.

The tournament announcer's voice crackled over the tannoy, talking about the abilities of the competitors, and how they reflected their day jobs. The rodeo is the only sporting contest in the world where work-day skills are tested in open competition. And they're big business – the Calgary

Stampede is just one part of a professional circuit that takes the competitors all over Canada and the United States. Competitors come from as far afield as Brazil, Argentina and even Australia, and the prize money can run into hundreds of thousands of dollars. Not here, though; here there wasn't any money on offer, only the traditional rodeo belt buckle awarded to the overall champion.

We listened intently as the announcer told us that if we were there for thrills and spills, we'd probably see a few. He added that what we were really going to witness, however, was something similar to a game of chess. 'It's not necessarily the move that is spectacular,' he said. 'It's the thought process that goes into it.'

We watched the first teams out there 'bulldogging' – where two cowboys go after one steer and rope both the head and the back legs, then get off their horses, haul the steer down and tie the legs together. It was fascinating watching the various competitors and the animals they were chasing; how some were a lot wilier than others. A few teams managed to get it done really quickly, whereas others made a small mistake and the steer took off in another direction.

Between the rounds, country music blared from the tannoy. You know the kind of thing: a croaky voice singing about how lonesome he is since his wife and dog ran out on him. It's the type of music that on any other day might make you contemplate suicide, but out there in the heat and dust, with the smell of the livestock, it was just as it should be.

The place was heaving and there was a real buzz in the air. There was no doubt that people looked forward to this event, where neighbours from different ranches could get together, drink beer and share war stories.

Down in the arena, I grabbed a seat next to an older, rake-thin cowboy called Eric. He was perfectly turned out in a striped shirt and Wranglers and a white straw Stetson curled up at the sides. He told me that this event had been running for twenty-five years now; it was a tradition that was entrenched in the community. He'd participated in the action plenty of times, competing on about fifteen occasions – back in 1995 he was on the winning team, and today he was wearing the massive silver belt buckle he'd won that day. He'd been particularly good at what they call team penning, which is when three cowboys use horses to separate, or 'cut', a group of cows from the herd and corral them. Cutting horses are generally a breed known as American Quarter Horses, renowned for their speed, and Eric told me there is good money in breeding them.

Early on we'd bumped into a team of girls, and we'd been rooting for them all day, because they seemed so nice and chatty, interested in who we were and what we were doing there. They'd done well with the team penning, but hadn't been so successful when it came to bulldogging. I asked Eric about the girls and he said they'd grown up on ranches with their brothers and were a match for any man when it came to a saddle horse.

Eric ranched five thousand acres just down the road, which was a pretty small outfit for this part of the country. He said that these days it was all he needed – he had a small herd and he didn't want to be leasing great tracts of crown land from the government. I asked him whether he farmed at all or if it was just cattle. Looking at me with his hat at a jaunty angle, he half smiled. 'Charley,' he said. 'I'll put it this way. I've never sold a bushel of wheat in my life.'

Back in Saskatchewan I'd asked Michael the same thing, and although, like Eric, he'd had a smile on his face, both men were pretty swift to point out that they were cattlemen and not farmers. Now I come to think of it, I seem to remember there was something in the Old West about range wars between ranchers and what were called 'sodbusters'. Anyway, this was *definitely* ranch country, and I could tell it was very much a community. It was clear that Eric knew the majority of the competitors, or at least their families anyway. He told me that the ranches tended to be handed down from generation to generation, and in this part of the country some of the family-owned places went back to the days of Canada's confederation.

While we were talking, the branding competition got under way. Eric explained that when the competitors roped the calf, they had to encircle both feet below the hock (which is sort of like the horse's elbow, if you can imagine that). If they only managed one, they were penalised. If they roped above the hock they would be disqualified. Turning to the elderly lady sitting next to me, who introduced herself as Rita, I asked her what she thought about it all.

'I guess it's just ranch work,' she stated. 'I guess it's what we do every day around here.' Rita's son was the organiser of the rodeo, and she told me that each team was sponsored, with the money going to the old school, now a museum – the Jasper Center – which needed money to redo its roof. It was a lovely idea – the whole town coming together, having fun and putting something back into the community all at the same time.

Eric and Rita were two stalwarts of Maple Creek and they were really lovely to talk to: old-school people with good values. Eric was very proud of the cowboy heritage, and was keen to emphasise that far from being dumb 'leather-arses', as they're sometimes known, the working cowboy or cowgirl is a real professional. He pointed to one guy competing in front of us who had been down at these same grounds only a few days before sorting a mass of cattle into different herds for breeding purposes. It is a skilled and sometimes dangerous job – animals are always unpredictable.

We took a wander through the lines of parked vehicles and horse trailers and found another great Western tradition: a bunch of contestants sitting in the sun with a cooler full of beer. They all wore hats, jeans and boots and most of them also had leather chaps on, as well as yellow competitors' vests. They all seemed fairly laid back, just sitting there waiting for their turn. Every member of a team has to take part in at least three events, though they don't all compete at the same time. It seemed that each year the members shifted from team to team, a bit like the transfer market in football.

I said it was nice to see them taking it seriously, making sure they were drinking enough beer. They told me that there were two things they needed to make the day work: fun and luck, and one tended to run into the other. They were currently lying fourth, but they weren't worried about it; in previous years they'd gone into the second half of the competition with only half a point but pulled out all the stops and won anyway. The events coming up were their specialities: cow milking, horse catching and the bronc riding. They seemed to be pretty confident.

Apparently the cow milking was the real spectacle of the day. 'That's when you want to get your pictures,' one of the guys, Alan, said. 'You see, Charley, one guy ropes the cow, another guy's mugging and the third has to get the milk.'

'Mugging?' I said. 'What's mugging?'

'That's when you jump on the cow's head,' he said, matter-of-factly. 'If you get a horn up your arse – whatever – you just have to go with it.'

Their cow-milking team consisted of Skinny, a hulking great guy in a black hat, Werbil, who was sitting on the bonnet of a truck, and Brutus, who seemed to be in charge of the cooler. Looking at them, I thought they'd probably do all right so long as it was Skinny doing the mugging. The milk was the key to winning the competition; they told me that a few years ago someone from another team had stolen their milk and it had made the front page of the local newspaper.

I really liked Alan. He was great fun with a really dry sense of humour. When we'd arrived this morning, the announcer had introduced him as the cowboy with the shortest legs in Canada and it's true he was pretty short, but according to Alan, the announcer was no taller than he was.

'It's OK,' he said. 'That bugger likes to mess with me, but I don't get mad, I get even. I'll find a way to get back at him before the day's out.'

'So how tall are you?' I asked him.

'Well,' he said. 'I was five one, but I think I'm about five foot now. You know, kind of shrinking with age.'

Leaving Alan and his team, I walked back to the arena, where I came across the team of girls we'd been supporting. They were pretty gutted that they had started so well and then fallen away. The competition was not over yet, though; they had the cow milking and were intent on making up the points they had lost so far. They were not that experienced, though, certainly not when compared with Alan's team; only one of their number had actually competed before. Having said that, this was stuff they did every day, and it was only the fact that people were watching, country music was playing and an announcer was introducing them to the crowd that changed anything. Get that out of your head and it was just like being on the ranch.

We were interrupted by the announcer, hoping that we were ready for some mayhem and wild activity. As far as I could tell, that mayhem was going to include me. Everyone seemed to know that I was due to ride a steer a little later, and I asked the girls if they had any tips for me.

'Sure,' one of them said. 'Keep your chest out, tuck your chin right in and grip as tight as you can with your legs.'

The cow milking was about to get under way. I was looking forward to this after everything Alan's team had been saying. As the first team walked their horses into the arena with their ropes at the ready, I went to get a better look. What I hadn't realised was that all the teams competed in the arena together, charging after their allotted target with hooves flying and dust kicking up, the cows getting the better of most of them. It really was mayhem: cowboys on horseback, others on foot trying to mug the cow while the rest dived for the flying hind legs. Sadly the girls came back empty-handed, not so much as a drop of milk in their bottle and their chances of winning disappearing into the distance. I loved the whole thing … the smell of the horses, the bawling of cattle in the pens, the crackle of static from the announcer's mike, even the country music. The atmosphere was just electric.

It was time for me to make my rodeo debut, and the nerves were beginning to kick in. What with the diving, the day training to be a Mountie and now this steer riding, I'd certainly done my fair share of nerve-racking things on this trip. Fortunately, there were lots of portable toilets dotted around the rodeo grounds, so I was able to have a last pee before I got on the steer. I hooked up with Skinny as he made his way over for the next event, the rowels of his spurs clanking as we walked past a stationary ambulance. I took a good long look inside, hoping they had everything I would need should I break any bones.

While Skinny and the other real cowboys would be

climbing on to a bucking horse, my cow was waiting for me in the chute. I stood there in my T-shirt, trainers and floppy sun hat, taking in how small the animal actually was. I'd probably be able to drag my feet along the ground.

Before I got on, the guys in charge of the bucking chutes gave me some coaching. They told me to take my wedding ring and watch off, then gave me a leather glove to put on my left hand. I insisted that I was right-handed. It didn't matter if I was right-handed or not; everybody used a left-handed glove. I guess it must've been something to do with being able to go for your gun ... but surely there were left-handed cowboys in the old days? Wasn't Billy the Kid left-handed? It didn't matter; the glove was for the left hand so it was my left hand I'd use. The trick was to have your hand between your legs, fingers gripping the rope, and ride on your hand, which added a touch more stability and some very necessary cushioning against the cow bucking beneath. My free hand should be up in the air for balance. I was nervous all right, but at the same time I was quite looking forward to it. I'd never done anything like this before, but then again, I'd galloped a herdsman's pony in Mongolia during *Long Way Round*, so how hard could this be?

I swapped my trainers for some boots and they tried to fit spurs on me, but for some reason they couldn't get them to attach properly. They told me that when I fell off, as I undoubtedly would, there would be somebody out there to make sure the cow didn't trample me. They fetched a pair of chaps and strapped those on while the announcer introduced me to the crowd.

'Ladies and gentlemen, we have a first-timer. He's travelled through Europe, Asia, Africa, Australia, and now he's part of a trip across the second biggest nation in the world ... We're talking Canada, we're talking extreme frontiers ... Ladies and gentlemen, Charley Boorman!' But that wasn't all. 'He's travelled Canada pretty much any which way he can: he might be motorbiking, he might be saddle-horsing, he might be hitch-hiking, but one thing I do know: before we get to the final event this afternoon, we're going to have him out here riding a cow!'

They gave me a body protector, which I was very glad of. The announcer continued to rattle on. 'We have us a motorbike-riding cowboy! They're even suiting him up with a hat.' And they did – little Alan's hat was plucked from his scalp and pressed down over mine. Russ stood by, getting the camera ready for the photos to go along with my obituary. I could see it now: 'Slightly famous adventurer trampled to death by small cow.'

They had what they call the tickle strap wrapped around the cow's belly now, and everything was ready. Suddenly, I didn't care that this was a cow. I climbed over that rail like

I really was Steve McQueen. Cowboys were all around me, the bell clanking away on the tickle strap as the announcer built up my part. Hands gripping the rail, I slid my legs down the steer's flanks, and the warm body of this beast was rippling beneath me. A cowboy worked the tie down around my palm as the announcer talked about me going down in a blaze of Canadian glory. Finally I was all set, and with one last look up at the others, I hooked my heels under the cow's belly. Then the gate was open and the animal was tearing across the arena ... and I was in the dust.

I think in bull-riding competitions you have to stay on for eight seconds. I'd lasted maybe one and a half. Before I had time to get my free hand airborne, I had slithered off the side and was eating dirt. Needless to say, I was on my feet in time to take the applause, then, hands aloft, I made my way back to the chutes. I was dusty but alive. I'd love to have done it again. A bit more practice and they'd get me on a saddle bronc.

In the meantime, the first of the real saddle-bronc riders was out in the arena, riding an unbroken Appaloosa that was doing everything in its power to buck him off. He hung on, though, and made the eight seconds before the pick-up guys – the cowboys on horseback who ride around the arena for safety –

came alongside and helped him slide off the bucking horse. My adrenalin was pumping just watching. I was really into this now, and I would have given anything to have a go. But that would have to wait for another time; right now it was the girls' turn, and we were really rooting for them. Only one member of the team would be riding. Kerry-Rae Joiner made her living exclusively on the back of a horse, and she was preparing herself to go into the arena now, one hand at her side flexing her fingers. I watched in awe as she climbed into the saddle – my little cow had been nothing compared to this. She rode a buckskin horse – that's tan with a black mane and tail – and she made the eight seconds before the whistle blew and the pick-up guys eased her off.

What a day! This was wild, fantastic fun and I could see why families had ranched in this area for generations. I was in awe of the competitors; I'd had just a tiny taste of the kind of buzz you get, and it was an experience I will never forget.

The next day was 4 July: Independence Day south of the border. We were back on the bikes and headed for a town called Drumheller. En route we passed through this small dot on the map, called Wayne. Riding along with the wind in my face, I noticed an old mine built into the hillside. I could see a car park, so obviously this was a place we could visit.

Mining in the area had been big business and Russ and I both knew we ought to take a peek.

Atlas No. 3 was a coal mine dominated by a massive wooden building that looked as though it was on its last legs. Criss-crossed with wooden walkways and covered gantries, it was built on the side of what was now a grassy green slope, though back in the day it was probably slag. For years the mine had played a vital role in the economy of the Drumheller Valley, providing coal for household use. I was introduced to the programme director, Jay, who was dressed like an old miner in a plaid shirt and dungarees with the requisite amount of coal dust on his face. He told me that the mine didn't officially close until 1979 and was the last of the 139 mines in the Drumheller Valley to cease coal production.

He led me up the long path to the old workings. It was a big operation even now, with something like 30,000 visitors a year. During its heyday, coal mining was the most dangerous occupation a person could have in Canada. There had been seventeen fatalities at this facility alone, but that was a relatively small number compared to other mines in the country. Jay told me of various disasters, including explosions of methane gas in which hundreds of men died. The deaths at Atlas No. 3 had been caused not by explosions, however, but by rock fall or something they called 'squeeze'. That was when the roof came down and the floor came up and those caught in between were crushed to death – a truly horrible way to go.

He took me into the tipple, an upward-sloping wooden tunnel laid with rails for the coal carts, which zigzagged its way right into the mountain. Apparently contract miners were paid according to the weight of coal they mined, and all of them were issued with brass checks with a number stamped on them. Jay showed me the number 57 check; if that was my number, my lamp would carry the same marking, as would my station in the washhouse and my ID tags. Each miner had a handful of tags with him every day; whenever he filled a coal cart he would place a tag on it, and when the cart arrived at the weighing scale the number was noted and that was how he would get paid.

The mined coal was tipped from the carts at the head of the tunnel on to a long conveyor belt that carried it down to what were called shaker screens – sheets of metal with various-sized holes in them that would shake 120 times a minute. That way the big pieces of coal would stay up top and the smaller chunks would fall through the holes to another shaker below. From the shakers the coal fell into hoppers, and was then shifted on to another conveyor belt, which ran out to the waiting box cars on the railroad below.

Standing there looking at the belt, I tried to think about what it would be like to have mined this mountain: the dirt and the dust, the airlessness, the threat of the roof caving in and the floor shifting always in the back of your mind.

Jay told me how the big chunks were treated with a combination of oil, wax and kerosene before they were dumped into the coal carts. The oil was to make the coal shiny and the kerosene to make it light up well in the fireplace, while the wax meant that they could paint the coal red. Red? What was he talking about? Both Russ and I were scratching our heads. Jay was clearly waiting for the question, so I asked it.

'Well,' he said, 'what colour is coal everywhere else in the world?'

'Black.'

'Right. So if you're the only one supplying red or orange coal, then people are going to remember you, aren't they?'

He went on to explain that they employed a teenager to sprinkle paint powder on the coal. All day, every day, that was what he did, going through pot after pot. The trouble was, in those days the paint was lead-based, of course, and people were cooking their food and heating their houses with coal that had lead sprinkled on it. Jay told me about one young coal sprinkler who fell ill and was diagnosed with lead poisoning. When he got better he went back to work, and told the managers what had been wrong with him and why; their response was that he should use a little less paint.

I asked Jay what it was like to be a miner back in those days, and he told me that it was pretty well paid for manual work – back in 1936, a contract miner could make ten dollars a day. The work was seasonal, though, with coal only being mined in the winter. The old hands brightened up their time playing pranks on the new guys. The miners would cut holes in the rock face so that the methane could escape. Apparently they told one new recruit that they needed to see if the hole was straight, so he would have to take a look inside. Unwittingly he obliged. The naked flame on his helmet lamp ignited the methane and he was blown off his feet and his eyebrows were scorched off. After that he was a marked man. According to Jay, the poor guy was the victim of prank after prank for the next few months.

Taking a moment to consider all the machinery, I realised that not only was it very claustrophobic in here, it must have been incredibly loud too. The conveyor belt would be going all the time, and the miners would have had to contend with the jarring rattle from the shaker screens and the coal falling through. Jay said it would have been non-stop, and of course in those days there was no such thing as ear defenders. Men regularly went deaf because of it.

At the top of the tipple, Jay showed me the elbow chute where the coal came down from the carts on to the conveyor. There were such massive quantities that the belt would clog up all the time and a young fellow would be there with a jemmy (a sort of crowbar) to unjam it. I spotted a sizeable weld where the metal had sheared; Jay told me that it was always a rush job to fix those because the welders would have been nervous about using a naked flame when the air was thick with coal dust and methane.

No miner was supposed to be younger than sixteen, but as Jay put it, in the old days age was negotiable, and from the records he knew of at least one person who had started at twelve. The younger you were, the worse job you got. One of the worst was 'bone picker'; a youngster who would stand at a certain point alongside the conveyor and pick out anything that wasn't coal: stuff like shale – what Jay called clinkers – petrified wood and, surprisingly, dinosaur bone. This place was chock-full of fossils apparently, and every now and again a chunk of T. rex that had been residing in the sandstone for seventy million years would be dug up with the coal.

I was itching to get underground. Once I was kitted out with lamp and helmet, Jay took me into the shaft and we walked up the steep slope to where the tipple connected with the mountain. By the time we reached the entrance I was pretty tired. After my exertions at the rodeo yesterday, and on the bike this morning, I was beginning to feel the days. We had been on the road for almost a month, but everything had been so varied that we hadn't really noticed the fatigue. There's a point on any expedition when the weariness just kicks in, though, and for a day or two every movement has to be forced. Walking into the mine, as thousands of miners had done before me, I was suddenly at that point. A little breathless, my limbs heavy – I imagined the others were feeling the same.

The moment we entered the mine, the temperature dropped. The deeper we went, the more certain I was that mining wouldn't have been for me. It wasn't just the cold; the tunnel felt tight and claustrophobic, although compared to some it was apparently quite wide. Jay mentioned the Sunshine mine, further south, where the tunnel was no more than two feet wide all the way along the seam. I couldn't imagine working in a space that narrow, but thousands did.

We went deeper still. The sandstone walls of the narrow shaft were supported by timbers and metal struts. Because it was sandstone, there was a little give, and that's why there was a danger of 'squeeze'. I could just imagine how terrifying it would be to find yourself trapped in here with the roof coming down and the floor lifting to meet it. Crushed to death and nothing you could do about it. I thought about Chile and the ordeal those miners went through, stuck at the bottom of that shaft for weeks on end while another shaft was sunk to try and rescue them. I'd only been down here a few minutes and it was enough already.

Outside again it was good to feel some air in my lungs. The view from the top of the mine was outstanding. High on the hill overlooking the valley, with the sun overhead, some of the fatigue I'd been feeling began to leave me. It got better still when Jay said I could drive the train. Before we went down, though, he pointed out a strip of highway in the distance and beyond it a couple of shacks. He told me that in the heyday of the mine there had been a town there with 200 houses, a hockey rink, hotel and store. It was nicknamed Cactus Flats, and when the mine shut down, the whole place was recycled and shipped over to a new location outside Calgary.

The 'train' I was driving was more of an engine actually, and a small one at that. I'd been imagining some steaming locomotive complete with cowcatcher and coal tender, but this was one of the old electric engines they used to take empty carts into the mine and bring full ones out. Pit ponies would bring the carts up from the deep, but once at the top, they would be hooked up to this engine. Since it was battery-powered, I assumed it was quite modern, but Jay said it actually pre-dated the serial numbers they had going back to 1936, so that made it at least seventy-five years old.

The engine was named Linda, with deference to mining

tradition, as all engines were given the name of some special woman – usually somebody's sweetheart. Jay said that Linda had been named after the executive director of the mine.

He showed me how to fire her up – to tickle Linda into life, so to speak – signalling first with the bell to let everyone know I was bringing her out of the shed. Once we were hooked up to some coal carts, Russ invited a few onlookers. Russ likes trains ... he likes trains *a lot*, actually. I'm sure he was keen to stop here because he knew that where there's a mine, there's a train. That didn't mean I was going to let him drive, though; no chance. Linda was my girl, and the seat at the wheel was taken.

10

Jurassic Park

The ride from Wayne was tough: very hot and sultry, the sun beating down to the point where the tarmac looked as if it was melting. A good night's sleep had done nothing to alleviate our fatigue and all the aches and pains. After a couple of hours' riding that sweating blacktop, we arrived in the town of Drumheller. In 1910, Colonel Samuel Drumheller had sunk the first mine shaft in the region here, which led to it eventually becoming the foremost coal-producing region in western Canada.

But Drumheller has another claim to fame. It just happens to be the dinosaur capital of the world, with the Royal Tyrrell Museum of Palaeontology housing the largest collection of fossilised bones in North America. You know you're in dinosaur country because as you roll into town you're greeted by a massive T. rex with all its teeth bared, towering above the tourist information office. Actually, T. rex and his friends are everywhere, with plaster dinosaurs jutting above shops selling fossils all the way down Main Street. We decided that we ought to drop by the museum and see if we could learn a little more about why this area was so important to palaeontologists.

Parking the bikes outside, we went to the desk and told them we were making a documentary about the extreme frontiers of Canada. There could be nothing more extreme than dinosaur country, so could they help us learn a little more? Of course they could! They were more than keen, and introduced us to the museum curator, François. He was a young guy – in fact he looked just out of university – but he was a researcher and palaeontologist and the top dinosaur man at the museum. We asked him why the area was so important, and he explained that only a mile north of the museum was a location known as the Albertosaurus bonebed – a layer of rock where the fossilised bones of thirteen Albertosaurus dinosaurs had been found. He showed us a scene they'd built to represent the landscape the dinosaurs would have roamed, complete with life-size models of these massive animals. They were awesome; each walked on its hind legs and had tiny little front legs and a huge head with rows of massive teeth – to me they looked a lot like T. rex.

When I mentioned that, François took me to another exhibit, the complete skeleton of an actual T. rex, intact and still in the rock. I was gobsmacked when he told me it had been found right here in Alberta. Some of the bones had been so badly damaged that they'd had to re-create them so they could show the skeleton. The pelvis, for example, was fabricated, and so was the head, although they did have the real head housed in a cool, dark place deep in the bowels of the museum. The rest of what I was looking at was real, though: the ribs, most of the legs and the tail. It looked huge to me, but François told me this was actually one of the smallest skeletons of a T. rex ever recovered. He described the way the bones were laid in the rock as a typical death pose for a meat-eating dinosaur, the head tipped back and the tail curled up.

He told me they were making new finds all the time; only the other day they had discovered an ancestor of the Triceratops that was eleven metres long. Apparently they were a rare find this far north; François believed there had been some environmental issues that made it more difficult for them to survive up here. When I was a young boy, Triceratops was my absolute favourite dinosaur, and I was wondering if there was any way we could go and see the dig for ourselves. Casting a glance at Russ, I knew he was thinking the same thing. We'd bide our time and wait for the right moment, see if François was up for it.

We wandered the halls, drinking it all in. I paused at one glass case where a dinosaur fossil lay curled on its side – Gorgosaurus, François told me, a distant relative of T. rex. This specimen had been found in an ancient river deposit, and François thought it was the currents that had curled the bones into the awkward position. It must've been preserved very quickly after it died, because all the bones were still connected, which is rare in any dinosaur fossil anywhere.

François became quite animated, telling me how much easier it is to put together a picture of what an animal would've looked like when you find a complete skeleton in one hit rather than bone by bone. I could tell he loved his job. *I'd* love his job – researching, making finds, putting on displays like this for the public. I could really get into that.

He took me to the prep lab, where the magic actually takes place. This was the really interesting stuff. God, I was in my element – the aches and pains of the rodeo, the tiredness all gone. I was like a kid in a sweet shop. A bunch of technicians were perched at various benches, working on new fossils that had just been brought in. They wore masks over their faces and were picking at the bones like surgeons, with massive cylindrical vacuum hoses suspended overhead to suck away the dust. François said they were peeling the fossils from the rock: painstaking work, because it's so easy to damage the bone as you're doing it.

I'd seen the smallest T. rex, and in another room François showed me the complete skeleton of one of the largest ever discovered; this massive meat-eating machine was twelve metres from head to tail, almost forty feet in old money. That's longer than a house is tall. Standing so close, I could feel a little shiver running down my neck; it's the size of these things that really gets the blood pumping. He also showed me the bones of another Gorgosaurus in the same death pose as the T. rex, and explained that originally it was thought that the bones were found like that because of the way the muscles withered and the ligaments shortened as the creature decomposed. Recently, however, scientists have started to believe that it's more to do with how they died, why they died, some kind of brain infection kicking in after the trauma, a shortage of oxygen that caused the skeleton to buckle that way. Mammals don't do that; it's only ever found in reptiles, apparently. It was fascinating stuff.

You forget just how long the dinosaurs were around for. For example, I had no idea that T. rex and Brontosaurus lived seventy-five million years apart. Did you know that? You watch *Jurassic Park* and they're all there together, but in reality there were millions of years between them. As much time separates us from T. rex as separates T. rex from those massive sauropods, the plant-eaters like Brachiosaurus.

We went into the workroom where they were taking apart the massive plaster casts that they encase the fossilised rock in so it can be transported back to the lab. I looked at one where the layers of burlap in the plaster had been peeled back; I could see rock complete with a set of teeth embedded in it. The tools the technicians use are pretty varied: scalpel blades, silk paintbrushes, toothbrushes and dental picks. They use glue to fuse the bones together as they start to prise them from the rock, because that way they don't crack and break off. It was fascinating to watch how they applied the glue with a syringe that allowed it to go into tiny cracks to shore up any damage before it actually happened.

I spoke to one of the technicians, Donna, who told me it's like a detective story. You find the fossilised rock in the field and think it's probably one thing, but as you start to work the fossil loose, to piece the bones together, you change your mind again and again, and by the time you've completed the task you've got something you had no idea about when you started out. A real journey of discovery; I loved that. It takes years to figure out what something is, to get it from its fossilised state into something you can identify for certain. There was an egg on display that had taken nine months to get from the rock to the point where they could put it on show. I thought that was pretty cool – a gestation period before it was brought back to life. Donna said that what blew her away was the fact that each time she did this, she was the first person ever to handle that particular artefact.

I commented that it must be a dream to work there. 'It is,' François replied. 'This is one of the best facilities of its kind in the world; all we have to do is cross the parking lot and we're in the Badlands and the fossils are literally everywhere.'

'Are they?' I looked again at Russ. 'Any chance we could see that for ourselves, François?'

It wasn't quite just across the parking lot; François fetched his truck and we started driving north. He was taking us to Horse Thief Canyon (those damn cowboys again), where apparently just walking through the valleys you could find bones poking out of the rock.

The museum vehicle was another great truck, by the way: a beaten-up Ford 250 twin cab, in white with accompanying rust. The view ahead was stunning: a series of flat-topped cliffs where the rock was exposed in overlapping layers. This place was only seventy-one million years old, which was quite a bit younger than the area where they found the fossils we'd been looking at in the museum.

Standing on the hilltop, I could see the canyon below

stretching for mile after mile, with layers and layers of rock apparent in the fractured hillside. This was where François and his colleagues came to play. He referred to the formation as a 3D exposure of the rocks, with each layer representing a different period in history. The layers were of various colours: white where rivers had flowed, for example, and black where coal had carbonised in the kind of swamps where the dinosaurs of the period liked to forage. The history of the earth was right there before our very eyes.

As we made our way down the slopes, we started to look for bones. I was following François, all of us on our hands and knees in the heat. I wasn't sure I could tell the difference between a stone and a fossil, no matter how many bones he said there were around here. It was exciting, though; I was on the hunt for dinosaurs. Finally François picked up something and passed it to me. 'That's a piece of dinosaur bone, Charley,' he said. 'Can you see all the little pores in it?'

I could see the tiny marks in the stone, but if he hadn't told me, I would just have assumed it was rock. It was amazing to be holding part of an animal that had roamed what would have been swamp land seventy million years previously. François passed me another piece with lichen growing on it. Lichen likes calcium, and even in seventy-million-year-old bones there is calcium.

A little further on, we found another piece of bone

embedded in the rock. This one was much larger, and I was really excited now. Donna gave me a brush so I could get rid of the dust that was coating it, then François and I scraped away the rock and dirt. I imagined unearthing this piece and then another and another until we had put together an entire skeleton. They told me it was a piece of broken tooth from one of the duck-billed dinosaurs, and I took a moment to sit back on my heels and gaze across the valley, thinking about that. This morning we had been in a mine, and now here I was with the curator of the Royal Tyrrell Museum, scraping dirt from the tooth of a dinosaur.

Talk about extremes: we'd begun our journey dipping a piece of twenty-thousand-year-old ice into our drinks, and here I was excavating seventy-one-million-year-old bones.

When I got back on the bike again that afternoon, I started thinking over all the experiences we'd had since landing at Cape Spear: the Vikings, the *Titanic*, diving the wrecks at Tobermory and riding off-road. I thought about paddling the Bloodvein and spending time in a First Nations sweat lodge. And now I'd been on a dig with the Royal Tyrrell.

Calgary was ahead, and having done one rodeo, we were arriving just in time for the world-famous Stampede. Back in Drumheller, we'd mentioned that we were headed this way, and they'd told us about a woman who would be taking part in what they called the 'extreme cowboy' competition. I wasn't sure what that was exactly, but apparently it's a mad competition, and, being into mad competitions, I was hoping to find her and persuade her to show me a few tricks. Well, to be honest, I wasn't sure I was hoping for anything other than a hot bath and a glass of Sancerre, but Russ had other ideas.

We parked the bikes outside the arena in Calgary As we made our way towards it, I could smell horses and cow shit. I cast my eye across rows and rows of livestock pens with lines of trucks backed up against them. Beyond the arena was downtown Calgary, with its skyscrapers and the Olympic Plaza. Up until the late 1960s, the downtown area was low-rise, but with the Arab oil embargo of 1973, Canada's oil became that much more important and buildings started to fly up.

The woman we were hoping to meet was Kateri Cowley, who worked her father Stan's ranch, not far from here. We asked for her at the gate and were told she was in the arena practising for the parade, so we made our way inside past the stock pens and the trucks. I'd been here before briefly with Ewan on *Long Way Round*, but we'd never really got this close. Up ahead a couple of cowboys were sitting on their horses, and beyond them a whole crowd of people were gathered.

They were rehearsing for the opening ceremony, galloping

up and down the length of the dusty arena. We saw Kateri canter past wearing a green shirt and a black hat. Eventually she rode up to say hello. She told us they were practising for the grand entry to what she called 'the greatest outdoor show on earth'. It sounded amazing, and it wasn't just for one night; the Stampede would go on for two weeks, and every night the grand entry would be the same, with a parade and fireworks – the whole nine yards.

Kateri told me that the extreme cowboy thing I'd heard about was actually what was known as the Cowboy Up challenge, where the rider has to showcase a variety of skills. If you've ever been on a ranch, you'll know the last thing you want anyone to say to you is 'cowboy up', because it means you're whining and not up to the task. Although it was the Cow*boy* Up challenge, Kateri was very much a cow*girl*, and she liked to be referred to that way.

'Look, Kateri,' I said. 'I know you're busy now, but later on will you teach me a few things? You know, roping and whatnot? I've ridden a cow so far, but that's all.'

She looked at me for a moment, and then she smiled. 'Charley,' she said, 'I'll make an extreme cowboy of you if it's what you want.'

'It's what I want,' I promised her. 'It's what I want.'

*

Later, after we had watched Kateri rehearse for a while, we met up with her outside in the car park and I followed her back to her father's ranch, the Rafter Six Ranch, a few miles outside of town. It was a huge place, with a massive wood-panelled Dutch barn with a shingle roof in the foreground. The backdrop was a series of staggeringly beautiful crags. What a place to live, what a place to grow up. I would kill for a view like that.

Beyond the barn, I could see a training corral; donning the black hat Kateri had given me, I made my way across. She was waiting with a rope lariat and a bullwhip, and a couple of horses – a skewbald and a dark-looking bay. One was saddled, one was not.

I can ride a horse, but I'd learned English style. The Western saddle is much bigger, and people say it's more comfortable, and easier, but I'm not sure. Like a gladiator, Kateri led me into the corral, and I mounted the saddled horse. She instructed me in the art of neck-reining, which allows the rider to keep once hand free for work, and I walked the horse around the corral and past a pen where the ranch stud – a beautiful black stallion with shaggy socks – was housed. He chased my gelding as far as his pen would allow. Then I was into a trot – or jog as they call it – my backside slapping the leather so hard I was reminded just how soft my motorcycle seat actually was.

Kateri told me she was going to test my skills, and then she was going to push them and see just what I could do. She warned she was ready to push me as far as I was prepared to go ... and then a bit further. A challenge then; I was up for that. 'So what shall we do first?' I asked her. She didn't answer; just hopped on the other horse bareback and told me I could keep my saddle for a bit but that it would be coming off later.

We trotted the horses, then cantered them around the corral. Kateri was better bareback than I was in the saddle. We both dismounted, and she strapped a pair of chaps on me and handed me a lasso. She explained that you need the loop to be as wide as the drop from your armpit to the ground. That's a big loop. The gap between the loop and the rest of the coils is called the spoke, and that needs to be about a third of the size of the loop. You have to swing the loop around your head with the back of your hand facing you, because otherwise it is going to buckle in on itself and then you have no loop.

It's much easier to watch than to do, I can promise you. On my first go I had my wrist position all wrong and got the loop out of shape. That led to the rope itself getting tangled, and I spent a long time missing the target. All I was trying to do was rope a static barrel. Meantime the horses were falling asleep, Russ and Nate were snoozing and Mungo had switched off the camera. There I was in the noonday sun, a mad Englishman trying to become a cowboy. It was really hard work, intensely frustrating, but finally I managed to throw a loop over the barrel, which had not moved all the time I was trying. If it was this difficult on foot, then how hard would it be on a horse, trying to bring down a running cow?

Kateri's skills had been perfected over the years, of course, although she was only twenty-six. She had grown up here and was twirling the rope every morning and every night, moving eighty horses from stable to pasture and back again. There is nothing easy about being a cowboy; it's some of the hardest work a body can do, and it's very poorly paid. I decided that you either have to just love roughing it, or you have to be born into it.

Next she taught me how to crack a bullwhip. That bloody whip! I kept whacking myself across the arse, the back, the back of my legs and finally across my neck and shoulders. At this rate I'd be flayed to the bone and we'd barely started with the horse. Kateri was brilliant, of course, cracking the whip back and front, from side to side and around her head, keeping it snapping the air. She was a lovely girl – all smiles and encouragement – but I wouldn't want to be alone with her and that whip if she was pissed off. No way.

Thankfully, though, she dispensed with the whip before I

lost an eye or worse, and we went back to the horses. I'm all right on a horse, and although I was riding bareback now, I managed to circle the corral at a canter. We saddled up again before we went for a proper ride, taking a trail that followed the river. Having proved myself to be the most inadequate cowboy on the North American continent, I was content to follow Kateri on a more gentle ride. Gentle, that is, until she told me we had to cross the river.

It was a big river – not very deep, maybe, but very wide, and with lots of rocks. It was also running pretty fast. As I followed Kateri into the water, I had an image in my head of the Big Muddy Lake and the roan mare leading all those stolen thoroughbreds across the shallows. I say it wasn't very deep, but out there in the middle it was up to the horses' flanks, and I had to keep my heels up. My horse seemed reluctant to make the crossing, the situation not helped when he decided to take a dump just as a group of rafters came paddling through. It was all worth it, though; I will never forget the view of the mountains from the middle of that river.

When we got back, Kateri hit me with the kind of invitation I would never have expected – especially after the way I'd fared with the rope and whip earlier. Friday was the grand opening of the Calgary Stampede, and Kateri Cowley, the eleventh best Cowboy Up challenger in the world, was asking me to join her in the first day's parade.

I couldn't believe it; not only were my skills about as cultivated as my way with words, but I also remembered that Kate and Wills would be in the audience. I was honoured, and not just because royalty would be there. Kateri had been to the stampede every year of her life, the first time when she was just a few months old. One year she had been the Calgary Princess, chosen from over thirty contestants. She'd spent a year of her life performing at rodeo events, speaking in public and promoting her home town abroad. She was an incredibly impressive person.

We watched Kateri put her horse through its paces, galloping up and down the field while cracking the whip, spinning the horse on its haunches as though she was barrel-racing. Finally she galloped up to us, braking hard, and as the horse dipped its head, she slid off the saddle and down the length of its neck. 'So I'll see you on Friday, then,' she said.

11

Three Thousand Metres
and Counting

While I was busy learning how to cowboy up, Russ had been making calls to see if we could find anyone who knew those impressive mountains behind the ranch well enough to give us a guided tour. This whole expedition was about challenging the frontiers, and it wasn't just about east to west and south to north; it was also about the peaks and troughs, and these were some of the tallest peaks in Alberta.

I was a little nervous about the idea – I'm no mountaineer – but it was totally in the spirit of what we were trying to accomplish. Late in the day, Russ told me he'd managed to get hold of Barry Blanchard, a local guide who was happy to meet us. So the following morning we were up early and off to a small commercial heliport on the edge of town to wait for him.

It was another great day weather-wise. The weather had been fine for a while now – gone were the grisly days we'd experienced on the east coast; this was the height of summer, and it was bloody hot.

When Barry showed up in a van, he turned out to be a genial guy. I'd been reading a little about him, and he really was a man of the mountains, with long grey hair tied in a ponytail. He'd trained a number of A-list film stars to climb for various movies; among others, he'd worked on *Cliffhanger* with Sylvester Stallone and *Vertical Limit* with Chris O'Donnell.

'So, what've you got planned for me, Barry?' I asked him when the introductions were over.

'Well,' he said, 'we'll take the helicopter – they fly climbers up there all the time – and once we find a decent place to land, we'll get you strapped into a harness and see if we can't find a way up the hill there.'

Hill? This was Mount Fable, the highest peak in the region, and as I put my helmet on, I couldn't help but wonder if it was 'fabled' for throwing climbers off. I was pretty nervous. As I said earlier, I was at the point where exhaustion was kicking in, and I'm not sure that's the state you want to be in when you attempt your first serious rock climb.

Arms folded, I looked at Barry doubtfully. 'You know I'm a complete novice? I mean, I've never really done this before, and right now I'm feeling very much outside of my comfort zone.'

'Don't worry about it. Comfort zones are designed for getting out of, and we were all novices once, Charley, think of it that way.'

All four of us were making the climb: me and Russ, Nat and Mungo. Barry was leading me, while one of the guides he worked with assisted the others with the cameras. As we lifted off, my stomach was churning. Climbing like this, high in the mountains, was a far cry from the little traverse I'd done the other day. I wasn't joking when I told Barry I was out of my comfort zone. I imagined he was well used to people telling him that; even so, I was experiencing plenty of butterflies as I looked out of the chopper window.

It was a hairy flight, although the helicopter pilot was very skilled; he flew in between the peaks where the sun was unable to melt the snow, and put us down in a gully where the ground underfoot was rock and shale. The crag massed grey above our heads, and the far slope was covered in pine trees. I wondered what kind of animals lurked there. We were way up in the boonies, and when the chopper left, the silence was immense. Hefting the backpacks, we started up the steep slope, with the shale shifting under our feet. It was still warm up here; I was only wearing a T-shirt and lightweight cotton trousers.

The 'trail' wasn't really a trail at all – the ground was loose and it sucked at our feet like sand. Hard on the calf muscles, hard on the lungs. I was puffing a little and we'd barely started walking, never mind getting up on the actual rock. Pausing for breath, I took a moment to consider our surroundings – the wall ahead looked flat and sheer and bereft of any hand- or footholds. I knew it wouldn't be like that when we got closer, but from where I was standing right then it looked pretty daunting.

The view was spectacular, though – the sweep of those crags, the tree-choked valley below. Barry told me we were between seven and eight thousand feet above sea level; that's five thousand feet higher than the highest point in the whole of the UK. I was breathless, really noticing the altitude and the way it depletes the air in your lungs. I was also nervous and excited, conscious that my safety depended now on Barry. I don't like being out of control, but if you're going to try this kind of stuff, then at times out-of-control is exactly where you're going to find yourself.

It looked a hell of a long way up, but Barry rested a hand on my shoulder. 'You don't have to worry, lad. The summit's up there and we're down here. All we have to do is get up there, then you'll have all kinds of stories to tell your grandchildren.'

'I hope.'

He laughed.

Hand shading my eyes, I was studying a crack in what I thought was the summit above. It was hard to tell from here; distances can be deceptive, and that might not have been the actual summit at all. 'So what's the route?' I asked. 'I mean, how do we do this?'

Barry was such a laid-back guy, taking his time, choosing his words, always a grin on his face. 'Oh, we'll mosey up there to the base of that chute,' he said. 'Then we'll get out some jangly bits and fix them into the rock and go one at a time.'

Barry was ready with the rope now, all the hardware clanking on his harness. Meanwhile, I was distracted by the fact that I'd been bitten by a mosquito. I couldn't believe it! You'd think the little buggers would leave a man alone way above the treeline, but no: no matter where you go in Canada, they're there ahead of you, just waiting to sample your blood. Barry reckoned that one or two had probably hitched a ride in the helicopter. They're sneaky like that, you know. Very, very sneaky.

Barry was totally self-effacing about his ability, but I have to tell you he's one of the great masters of his craft, and we were just so lucky to find him. He's renowned as one of the best alpine climbers in North America, and he made the first ascent of a route called the Andromeda Strain here in Alberta. Mountaineering, it seemed, was very much in the family; Barry had met his wife Catherine while making an ascent of a small hill called Mount Everest.

We began the ascent – that's a technical term, by the way – the trail of shale and rock getting steeper and steeper. I followed Barry, head down, toes digging in to keep my balance. It was hard going, and very hot. The walk seemed to go on for miles, though in fact it was only a few hundred feet. With the way the other peaks fell away all around us, I really did feel we were pushing the frontier.

From the shale, we moved on to solid rock; it was steeper here, with big boulders to clamber over, though we still weren't using the ropes yet. I was puffing and blowing, my T-shirt sticking to me. I made sure I was watching Barry closely, placing my feet where he was placing his and using the handholds he selected for balance. Finally we were approaching the bottom of the route itself, and shading my eyes once more, I looked up. 'Oh my God,' I said, 'that is steep.'

We were on shale again now, and we used ski poles as walking sticks to help us. We climbed on and on until finally the loose stuff was left behind and we had reached water-worn limestone. Barry said that the water was slightly acidic, and the calcium carbonate in it changed the colour of the stone. Part of the cliff face was grey and other parts looked almost yellow; apparently that was because the yellow sections were not getting hit directly by rain, which meant they were much steeper. 'Let's steer clear of the yellow bits, then, shall we?' I suggested.

I would not be that lucky. Part of our route would take us on pitches that stretched across those really steep sections. I was reminded how dangerous climbing could be when I took my helmet off to wipe the sweat from my eyes. Barry told me to make sure I placed it on the ground with the top facing up, which was what he called 'Happy Turtle'. Upside down was 'Sad Salad Bowl', because it was more likely to tumble down the mountain and then I would have no protection when a rock fell on my head. Happy Turtle, then, I'd remember that, because I'd promised my wife that this wasn't going to be dangerous.

We climbed right up to where it was cooler, single file. All I could see was Barry's butt just a few inches in front of my face. We really were high now; if we'd been at eight thousand feet back where we started, then where the hell were we now? It was awesome, but the really difficult bit was yet to come. The higher we climbed, the closer the sheer stuff got, of course: it seemed to grow and grow until the wall of rock dominated everything. Around us were ridges, saddles of other slopes, but this was the tallest by far. It was unbelievable, truly incredible, and forgetting my nerves for a moment, I became quite emotional, so much so that there were actually tears in my eyes. It was so beautiful, a wonderful experience to be up that high looking out over the backbone of this amazing country. Suddenly I could understand why climbers do what they do.

A few metres higher and we were into a narrow chute. Roped together now, we started picking our way up the channel. My mouth was dry and I was concentrating only on where I was placing my hands and feet. Barry was just above me, pausing now and again to look back and make sure I was all right. I was waiting until he'd negotiated each section before I followed. As we approached the sheer rock face, Barry prepared the belay. A belay is where you climb 'lead' and 'second', with one of you securely fastened. I would 'second', feeding the rope to Barry as he made the pitch, using cracks in the rock for the 'jangly bits' – what climbers call the 'protection' – and clipping the rope to them with karabiners so that if he fell I would hold him. The protection in the wall forms a pivot point to break the fall, the weight of which would be on me. That's the basic principle of rock climbing: one at a time, pitch after pitch, the lead guy getting so high then tying off while his partner ascends and removes the bits and pieces of protection from the wall.

We were scything a path up that face, and I was conscious of every hold. Barry was brilliant, so calm and collected, pointing out the route and encouraging me all the time. It was a nerve-racking, exhilarating business, but I felt in safe hands and knew that he wouldn't put me in harm's way. Coming up after him was really tough; with the lead guy already belayed on the next section, you're on your own looking for the holds, removing the gear and trying to stop the rope getting caught in the cracks. I was scared, panicky, uttering a never-ending litany of expletives that I won't print here. From being exhilarated and fully cognisant of why people do this, I was suddenly terrified. High up in the middle of nowhere on the end of a rope: what the hell was I doing here?

Russ was above me; he had already made this pitch so that he could take some photos, and as I approached one section I couldn't fathom, he shouted encouragement from above.

'Holy shit,' I called back. 'How do you get up this bit?'

'You've got to swing your leg up,' Russ told me. 'There's a foothold, Charley. Just swing your leg up.'

Finally I made it to the ledge above. This was a lengthy traverse where there were no handholds, only the lip for your feet, with your body pressed against the wall. It was more of a shuffle than a climb, easing my way across with my breath tight and sweat rolling off my brow.

Taking the protection out was easier said than done; there was one particular metal wedge that Barry had hammered into the rock, and the only way to get it out was to whip the sling it was attached to upwards. The trouble with that was that I was on a ledge, God knows how many feet above the ground, and every time I tried to whip the wedge out, I lost my balance. I cannot tell you how unnerving that was. Try as I might, I just could not get it out. I left it. Barry could retrieve it later.

That part of the climb was really tough, but when I did get some purchase under my feet, and with it a little of my confidence back, I had the presence of mind to mess about for the camera. With one foot on the ledge, I grabbed a handhold and swung round, trying to do my best *Cliffhanger* impression. It soon got serious again, though, as above the ledge we were into another steep ascent, following a crack that ran from the bottom of a ten-metre slab. It was hard not to get your feet stuck, and I had an image of that guy in Utah climbing on his own ... Danny Boyle turned the story into that film, *127 Hours* ... yeah, that one where the boulder shifts and his arm gets stuck and he uses a penknife to cut it off. Anyway, onward and upward. This was as tough as anything I'd ever done and I really was out of my comfort zone. But I had no choice but to go on. You can't give up on a rock-climbing route, it just isn't an option, so I gritted my teeth and carried on swearing to myself. 'It ain't pretty, Barry,' I called, 'but I'm coming.'

Beyond the crack, it got even worse. We were on a saddle – a really narrow ledge – roped together but using no protection. We were walking this narrow strip of loose rock, with the world falling away on both sides, and that totally freaked me out. It was bad enough on the ledge or ascending the crack, but with no wall to hold on to, just this sort of humpbacked bridge, it was absolutely terrifying. You could tell how bad it was because while Barry was walking upright, holding the rope, I came scrabbling along after him on hands and knees like some sort of reluctant dog.

The trouble with approaching the summit is that all around you everything just falls away. That last ridge was the worst, and even standing on the top, having accomplished what we'd set out to do, I wasn't full of the

With cowgirl Kateri Cowley at the Rafter Six Ranch in Alberta.

Kateri rode her horse bareback better than I did with a saddle, but I didn't do too badly in the training corral. At least until we started the rope work . . .

Riding through the Canadian wilderness with Kateri is an experience I'll never forget – I felt like a real cowboy.

The Rocky Mountains were a frontier we had to explore, but even with our expert guide Barry Blanchard to help us, the climb was one of the most challenging things we did on the trip.

Still a long way to go. Barry and I assess the route ahead.

We made it! Team Extreme Frontiers at the top of Mount Fable, nearly three thousand metres up.

Russ making sure Extreme Frontiers leaves its mark on Mount Fable.

An enormous ice-road truck on a decidedly un-icy road in Inuvik, Northwest Territories.

Russ and I battle against the mosquitoes in Tuk, Northwest Territories.

There's gold in them thar hills. Panning for gold in the mining town of Dawson City in the Yukon.

Arriving on the Discovery Ice Field for my 'escaping from a crevasse' training!

Canada really does have some of the most beautiful scenery in the world, and we were lucky enough to see more of it on our way to the crevasse.

Lowering myself – voluntarily! – into the crevasse with my guide, Sian, watching from above. She made getting out again look easy, but I doubted it would be so simple.

Getting a few gliding tips from pilot Rudy.

Gliding high above the hills in British Columbia with Rudy. Moments later he would take the glider into a loop-the-loop . . . and my stomach would do the same!

What goes up . . .

. . . must come down.
On foot. After tumbling off my bike,
we walked them over a particularly
icy part of the route.

Hurtling down the mountain on a push-
bike was exhilarating, but my first love will
always be the motorbike.

Going underground. We'd been east,
west, north and south, 3,000 metres up
and now we were 70 metres below at
the Horne Lake Caves on Vancouver
Island. We really had pushed every
frontier Canada had to offer.

Leading a convoy of Canadian bikers into Tofino on Vancouver Island – the western-most point of our trip and the end of this Extreme Frontiers journey.

The Extreme Frontiers team (Mungo, Russ, me and Nat) at the end of the road. For now.

achievement so much as wondering about getting down. Climbing up is one thing, but when you get there you still have to go down, and I've heard people say that that is much harder. I was terrified and at the same time in awe of people like Barry who do this for fun. But the fact was, I'd done it. I'd never rock-climbed before, and yet I'd made it to the top of Mount Fable, and that was a real achievement. When the nerves finally settled down, I made sure I congratulated myself, then congratulated Barry and thanked him for getting me up there.

We camped on the summit, planning to sleep out in our bags. Russ was lying on his sleeping mat reading an old Penguin classic, *The Last Frontier*, which seemed pretty appropriate. As we chatted, he told me, in that quiet way of his, that he'd not realised the climb would be so challenging. Challenging? It was bloody terrifying, especially that last ridge. I could still feel it now. Russ agreed, admitting that that part had been pretty hairy, with nothing on either side and the knowledge that if you slipped, you'd fall to what would be certain death. Not a nice thought, but when you don't fall, when you make the summit, it's a fact that the feeling of achievement couldn't be re-created anywhere else.

'What's really cool is that the four of us did it together,' Russ told me. 'It's the biggest challenge we've had so far, the top of a mountain, Charley; that's a first for all of us.'

Having said that, the thought of climbing all the way down again was not one either of us relished, so Russ asked Barry if we could organise a helicopter to pick us up in the morning.

As I said, the plan had been that we would sleep under the stars, but with rain clouds massing, we pitched the tents after all. Evening was drawing in, and having got over the fear I'd felt on that last section, I realised that this experience was right up there with anything I had ever done. I mean it; other than marrying my wife and seeing my children born, this was just about the most amazing thing I had ever been part of.

I slept a little, but woke at about 1.15 to the most amazing storm. Thank God we'd brought the tents, because it was blowing a gale now and the sides were rattling away nineteen to the dozen. That's the thing about mountains: on a perfectly sunny day there can be a sudden snowstorm that can lock you in for days.

Fortunately there was no snow and we weren't locked in. By five in the morning we had packed up the tents and were ready to go. The clouds were lower than ever, though, and with the wind swirling, the landing site for the chopper was a mass of flying stones. He came, though, our bush pilot, bringing salvation from the skies, flying in with the wind buffeting the fuselage, rocking the whole ship from side to side. He couldn't wait long, so no sooner had the skids touched down than we loaded the gear, clambered aboard and got the hell out of there.

12
Ice Road

We got back very early in the morning, which was just as well, as I had to take my place in the opening ceremony of the Calgary Stampede. I'm not going to go into too much detail about it here, because I've already described my part in one, albeit slightly less glamorous rodeo. All I'll say is it was very cool to be there with the Duke and Duchess of Cambridge in attendance, part of the greatest outdoor show in the world.

Thankfully, after all that excitement, I got plenty of much-needed sleep that night, and on the morning of 9 July we started out on one of the most glorious drives you can make anywhere in the world. I say drives, but of course I was on two wheels as we rode from Calgary up the Icefields

Parkway. It is like nowhere else on earth. The road twists and turns through forests and open grasslands into a panorama of lakes and glaciers from Lake Louise all the way to Jasper and the Columbia Ice Field beyond. I was delighting in the fact that I wasn't on a horse or a cow but a motorbike; two glorious wheels under me, or just the one now and again when I had a mind to pop a wheelie. I wasn't halfway up Mount Fable, clinging on for dear life, or in a narrow mineshaft thinking about the squeeze. I was in the great outdoors, doing what I like doing best, and I was revelling in it. Mile after mile just unfolded in front of me, and I was really in the zone, until a sudden movement in the valley caught my eye. Something was moving down in a grove of maple trees deep in the canyon – some sort of animal. Pulling over to the side of the road, I took a moment to figure out what it was.

A black bear foraging for berries. I could not believe my eyes! A black bear, and only about seventy yards away. I'd never seen one in the wild before. Black bears can be dangerous, but they're more docile than their brown cousins and much more likely to run from humans than get into a fight. This guy was beautiful, just moseying around in the brush, chewing at this and that, minding his own business while the traffic zipped by on the road above. We had to press on, though, so clipping on my helmet, I started the bike again. As I roared away, the bear looked up, a little nonchalantly.

Ahead of us was the ice field. I'd heard that you can visit the glacier in these incredible vehicles, sort of coaches, I suppose, with tyres as tall as I am. When we arrived, a couple of the coaches were parked in bays, and having located a young guy called Jason, I asked him if he would take us up to the field.

'This is for TV, right?'

'Yes, a show called *Extreme Frontiers* that's going to be shown back in the UK.'

'I tell you what, then,' he said. 'Rather than me take you, why don't *you* take me? I've heard you're up for different vehicles, isn't that right?'

I was gobsmacked. 'Really?' I asked. 'You mean I can drive?'

'Yeah, why not?'

'OK then.' I didn't need to be asked twice. 'Let's do it.'

Jason worked for Brewster Ice Explorers, who operate these unique snow-coaches, taking guests on what is called the Columbia Icefield Glacial Adventure across the Athabasca Glacier. The area around Mount Columbia is unique – it's what's known as a hydrological apex, where the glacial meltwater feeds rivers that pour into the Arctic Ocean as well as both the Pacific and the Atlantic. It's one of the largest accumulations of ice south of the Arctic Circle, covering more than 300 square miles.

Getting behind the wheel, I asked Jason who had made the snow-coach, and he told me it was a company called Foremost down in Calgary. They had taken the best design elements from its two predecessors to build the vehicle I was driving now. Like everything else up here, the modes of transport seemed to be constantly evolving. Sitting there looking at the switches, and the old-fashioned steering wheel, I felt like I was in the old London bus on the first stage of my *By Any Means* expedition. Two levers operated the doors, one to lift the steps you needed to climb inside and the other to actually close the doors. Disengaging the parking brake, I found the gear shift and put it into reverse. Jason told me that the key to driving these coaches was to turn the wheel early, as it had a very large radius and took a while to spin round.

There are only twenty-three such coaches in the entire world – twenty-two operating here in the Canadian Rockies, with the other being part of the US government's research programme in Antarctica – and they cost $1,200,000 each, so I was really privileged to be behind the wheel. And it actually wasn't that hard – the gears were simple to work out and the steering was power-assisted. Unfortunately, the hill out of the loading area is one of the steepest around, and that's what I had to negotiate first. It was a dirt road, and God only knows what the gradient was. Sitting behind me, though, Jason was able to gauge how I was doing, and within a couple of minutes he was offering me a job.

The tyres were pretty soft, and they covered the rugged terrain really well. I'd seen a picture back at the base where the glacier was almost up by the road, but it wasn't like that now. Jason told me that the ice had been receding since 1834, and since then it's lost about 70 per cent of its original mass. Right now it was losing ten metres or so a year, though the reasons for that are still up for debate. When he's taking tours, Jason tends to avoid the subject, because people have strong opinions about whether or not global warming is to blame. He said that over the years they'd had many different glaciologists up there taking readings and doing research; about half of them said the shrinkage was because of global warming and half that it was just a natural phenomenon.

They have lots of climbers visiting the area, particularly in April and May when there is still plenty of snow on the ground and they can make their way up to the ice field very easily. There's a debate, of course, about whether vehicles such as this snow-coach should be driving up the glacier at all, but Jason pointed out that it was safer to have organised tours than just letting people cross willy-nilly. The glacier is potentially a dangerous place, with crevasses that you could fall into and mill wells where water drills holes deep into the glacier. They're avoidable, of course, but you can't always see them, as for much of the year they're covered with snow.

I knew all about that, because one of the things Russ had planned for me later was a glacier rescue, where I would fall in and have to rescue myself. When I told Jason about it, he thought it was a novel idea, as in his experience, people who fell into a glacier rarely made it out. Glaciers can be very deep and you could be falling for a long time. But more of that later; right now I was driving this incredible bus in this absolute wilderness, and I was enjoying every minute. The truth is, I'm never happier than when I'm behind a steering wheel, and this was one of those incredible vehicles which you just tick the box for and say, yep, been there and done that: a snow-coach on the Columbia Ice Field in Canada.

The glacier is on a V-shaped cleft and the safest way to traverse it is right through the middle. That's where the ice is deepest, and deep ice isn't so prone to cracking as the shallower stuff. It's not foolproof, mind you, and it is vital that the road is well-maintained and regularly inspected for cracks, crevasses and mill wells.

The glacier opened up on either side of the road, white, grey and shades of yellow, cutting a swathe through the gorge. Passing another coach on its way down, we got some odd looks from the tourists; I imagined they were thinking I'd stolen the vehicle and was heading for the hills like a latter-day Dutch Henry or something.

'Trouble is, you wouldn't get very far,' Jason told me. 'This thing only does eighteen kilometres per hour. I could run and still catch up with you.'

We went as far as the coach could go, and then got out on to the glacier itself, which is six kilometres in length and a kilometre across at its widest point. Beyond it lies the actual ice field, and that is the size of the city of Vancouver. We all drank straight from the freezing meltwater – it was crystal clear and as fresh as anything I'd tasted. Jason told me that the turnaround point is the deepest part of the glacier; the ice beneath our feet descended some 300 metres. That's as deep as the Eiffel Tower is tall, so it's a lot of ice. The coldest temperature ever recorded up here was minus 52 Celsius without wind chill; that's way colder than I wanted to experience. Not a place to get trapped in the middle of winter.

*

We said our goodbyes and thanks to Jason, then we rode the bikes on to Edmonton where we hopped on a plane to Norman Wells in the Northwest Territories. Having explored the border with the United States, I was itching to dip a toe in the Arctic Ocean.

We only waited in Norman Wells long enough to get the next plane, which took us further north to the town of Inuvik, part of the ice-road system that criss-crosses Canada. Having been involved in driving Dalton Highway in Alaska earlier in the year for a television programme on the world's most dangerous roads, I was dying to meet some truckers so I could compare experiences. A couple of hours later we were on the ground in bright sunshine, making our way across the apron to the small airport building. The plan was to spend the day in Inuvik, then fly on tomorrow to a traditional Inuit village, where they hunt beluga whale to feed them through the winter.

We'd been booked into a really neat little hotel – it was more of a lodge really, with individual log cabins – and we dumped our bags there before heading off to explore the town. It wasn't very big, just a handful of single-storey buildings clustered around one road, with a population of a little over 3,500 people. Those people (as we had found everywhere we'd been so far) were very friendly – happy to chat and keen to know what we were doing up here. I wondered what it would be like to live here, with two months of the year in total darkness and another two when it stayed light all the time. Wandering up Main Street, we found the Café Gallery – a busy little place with a long counter and a handful of tables. We ordered coffee and some sandwiches, and took a moment to regroup and think about what lay ahead.

The Dempster Highway, more than 480 miles long, runs from the Klondike Highway in the Yukon up to Inuvik on the Mackenzie River delta. It's a famous road, attracting a real variety of people. At the café we met a German riding the highway on a motorbike, but people do it on pushbikes, and some even hike the entire length of it. In winter, the road up here is permafrost – solid ice – and the town is a stopping point for the men and women who drive those absolutely massive commercial trucks. We hadn't come across any drivers yet, but after we'd eaten, we did find a place off the main drag called Northwind Industries, where they service the big trucks. They need a lot of maintenance, because they have to travel 800 kilometres of dirt road before they hit the first tarmac, and from there it's another 1,600 to the company's depot in Edmonton. I chatted to Aidan, a nice guy who ran the Inuvik depot. He told me how the terrain is tough on the vehicles; the trucks just tear through tyres. On one recent construction job they went through fifty-four tyres in only the first week.

Outside, I took a look at one of the smaller trucks: a long-bonneted beast being worked on by a guy in a cowboy hat named Guy Philippe. I was really intrigued by his accent – it still had the American twang but was definitely influenced by French. Down south, listening to the cowboys talk, we could have been in America – apart from the odd word like 'bugger' and the way they pronounced 'out' (more like 'oot'). Over on the east coast there was the Irish influence I'd noticed.

Guy was repairing the hydraulics that worked the truck's tipping mechanism, welding in a new plate at the base, and sparks were flying everywhere. It was an easy enough task with the sun shining, but I wondered what it would be like in the long, harsh winter when the temperature was fifty below. He told me he came from Ottawa, so perhaps that explained his accent. He said that there were not that many heavy-duty truck mechanics around any more, and not that many drivers either, because younger people had no interest in that kind of work. He'd only been in Inuvik for four months, but he had experience of the climate and knew exactly what he was in for come the winter. The trucks would get iced up, and when they started to thaw, the water would drip all over the mechanics working on them. I couldn't think of anything worse than trying to fix something on one of those vehicles while ice water seeped through your clothes.

Trying to keep a massive truck running is far more difficult than a car; everything is twice the size, three or four times the weight and far more awkward. Add to that the extreme temperatures, and it's not something I could contemplate, that's for sure. But it was exactly what this guy enjoyed doing: all his working life he'd been a mechanic, and he liked nothing better than getting wet and dirty. He didn't mind the cold either. He told me that being a mechanic up here was just like playing with Tonka toys when he was young, only now the toys were a little bigger.

Aidan showed me around the inside of the workshops, where a massive twin-cab pickup, jacked up with winter tyres, was parked. It was a colossal Ford 350, with bull bars and as many additional headlights as you could shake a stick at, and it was nicknamed Little Pig. He indicated another huge vehicle that looked a bit like the snow-coach I'd been driving at the Columbia Ice Field; this was designed to go under the tundra and carve out an ice road. He also showed me snow ploughs that could shift drifts thirty metres wide, explaining that you couldn't allow the snow to bank up on the side of the road, because it would drift again every time the wind blew.

This area is oil-rich, and Northwind Industries' trucks are used to ship out the sludge that's brought up by every drill bit; they transport it 2,000 kilometres south, where it can be treated and dumped effectively. Aidan told me that one of his vehicles was just south of town on the weigh scales right now, and he could take me down to have a closer look. Finally, I'd meet one of the drivers I'd been hoping to talk to. Maybe I'd get to ride along part of the Dempster Highway.

Inuvik is a pretty ramshackle place, and as we left town I saw lines of trailer homes and small wooden houses with pickups parked outside. Although it gets cold here, they don't have the extreme conditions experienced in the villages up on the coast, where a blizzard can last an entire week.

As soon as we pulled into the weigh station, we saw the truck, complete with twin trailers snaking out behind. Aidan had radioed ahead and told the driver to hang on because he had a couple of passengers arriving. The driver's name was Mike (another one), and he waited, engine idling, as we climbed into the cab. I shook his hand and asked him how long he had been doing this job.

'I've been driving trucks for twenty-some years,' he said.

'But I've been five years up here. I did two winters in Tuk and a winter in Norman Wells before that as well.'

I commented that it must be a lot easier driving in summer, when there's no ice on the ground, but he shook his head. 'Not really,' he said. 'In summertime the road is dusty, dirty; you get soft spots and that plays havoc with the tyres. Yeah, you got the snow and ice in winter, but when the temperature is forty below zero, it's not that slippery. I've spun out a few times, I guess, coming back and forth up this highway, but most of it is in the springtime or early fall when the snow's either melting or just arriving.'

Mike had seen his share of accidents, and with only one ambulance for 750 kilometres of highway, it is not the place to crash your vehicle. With the highway being so potentially treacherous, the truckers stay in contact on the radio, letting one another know where they are, so that if anything happens they're not quite as isolated. As Mike pointed out, most accidents happen in the summer – probably because in winter the only people on the road are the truckers, and they know what they're doing. When there are a lot of tourists around, anything can happen; apparently they have a habit of stopping right in front of you if they catch a glimpse of wildlife in the brush.

Mike told me that halfway along the highway is Eagle

Plains, where there is a gas station and hotel. The area around it is known as Hurricane Alley. The road there is gated, and if the wind is blowing hard, they close the gates. The traffic then backs up and nothing moves until the storm clears. The longest Mike had had to wait there was some six or seven days. He didn't mind; it was part of the job: the round trip from oilfield to the plant where the toxic sludge is treated takes five and a half days even if everything goes well. He stays in the truck all that time, eating and sleeping in the forty-two inches of living space behind the seats, and taking showers at the truck stops along the way.

Mike has a fifteen-year-old daughter who lives in Grand Prairie, Alberta. One of the reasons he decided to take this job was that he drives through the town on every trip. The work is also very well paid – Mike reckoned that if he did the same thing in a place like Edmonton back down in Alberta, he would earn thirty to forty thousand dollars less than he does up here. On top of that, an ice-road driver only works eight or nine months of the year and the rest of the time is his own. In a good year, he rakes in over a hundred thousand dollars, and that's not too shabby.

But the Dempster is not a highway for the 'average person', as Mike put it. A truck driver is responsible for his vehicle, his load; the 'weak of heart' don't belong on the road. He was right: with the varying conditions – the soft patches in summer and the sheet ice in winter – it can kill you in a heartbeat. Looking through the windscreen, I could see the way the highway unravelled before us, mile after mile of nothing but mind-numbing, arrow-straight dirt road and stunted-looking trees.

It might sound like a boring job, but no day is the same for Mike. It's 190 kilometres from Inuvik to Tuk over the ice, and one job he did out there was on an ice field that extended another 140 kilometres out into the frozen McKinley Bay. He took some photos of that trip, his truck parked next to a ship that was frozen in the ice, with an offshore rig sitting opposite. One year when he thought they had finished for the season, his boss told him there was one final job, hauling gravel north for a road they were building in Tuk. This was two weeks into April, and by the time they were finished, there was two or three inches of water on the ice road all the way back to Inuvik. When Mike got back, he and another driver were asked to collect a truck that had broken down in Yellow Knife; as they crossed the last river, the trailer was in four feet of water. I asked him what he thought of the TV series *Ice Road Truckers* and he just looked at me and smiled. 'American TV ...' he said. 'Like everything else, it's blown way out of proportion.'

'You mean all the drama and accidents?'

'It happens now and again, but most of the time this is just like any other job, I suppose.'

I tried to persuade him that driving a truck carrying 56,000 kilos of load, plus the weight of the truck and trailer, on six feet of ice was anything but 'just like any other job'. He thought about that, and conceded that maybe I had a point after all.

13
Chuck in Tuk

We spent the night back in Inuvik (where we just about managed to keep the bugs out of the room), and at first light we were up and making our way to the airport, where a young pilot named Kelly was waiting to fly us to Tuktoyaktuk, or Tuk as everyone calls it. The plan was to camp out with an Inuit family on the shores of the Arctic Ocean. I was praying the mosquitoes wouldn't follow us that far north.

Somehow I had managed to lose the bag containing all of my camping gear – like an idiot, I'd left it at the lodge. Kelly told us not to worry. This wasn't the only flight she was making today; she would collect my bag and bring it up for me later. That sort of kindness was typical of this part of the world. Canada may be the second largest country on the planet, but with only about twenty-five million people, it feels like one big family. So, knowing I'd have my sleeping bag for later, I was able to sit back in the small plane without worrying.

Russ wanted to know if I was going to swim in the Arctic Ocean – he felt we should all do it, have a team experience so to speak, and he asked Nat what he thought.

'I don't know about the team experience,' Nat said. 'But I'll take a dip.'

Mungo suggested we go buck naked. Russ thought that might be quite liberating. I wasn't so sure.

'Don't worry about it,' Russ said. 'It will be so cold there'll be nothing to see and nothing even vaguely macho about it. But I think we should do it; after all, this is our third frontier, and how many people can say they've swum in the Arctic Ocean?'

In the summer you can't drive as far as Tuk, as the 'road' is actually a river delta and it needs to be frozen over before vehicles can travel on it. When the ice has melted you have to go by plane or boat, and as we were flying in, the plan was to come back down the river the next day with a local Inuit called Chuck, who had promised to show us around. It was his pal we were camping with tonight.

Kelly had warned us that the flight might be a little bumpy, but thirty minutes after leaving Inuvik we landed with no disasters. The airport, such as it was, was not far from the tiny town, which straddled a couple of low-lying islands connected by a dirt road. Most of the buildings were low, wooden structures, more like cabins than houses, dotted along the flat and featureless peninsula. For many years the town had been known as Port Brabant, but in 1950 it was renamed Tuktoyaktuk – the first place in Canada to be given a traditional First Nations name.

On the airstrip Russ noticed the drop in temperature and he asked Kelly if that meant we'd finally be free of mosquitoes. No such luck. Kelly told him there were actually plenty of mosquitoes, especially at this time of year, and if we were camping, we might want to invest in lots of spray and nets to wear around our heads. What? I couldn't believe it! The mozzies had been pretty awful ever since we got here, but never so bad that we needed to wear headgear. This was the Arctic, for God's sake; what were mosquitoes doing way up here? Tuk is actually inside the Arctic Circle, and is one of the most northerly settlements anywhere in the world!

Chuck was waiting to meet us, and he happily ferried our gear over to his place. It really was pretty cold up here, colder than most of the places we'd been, and it cut through our clothes. Now that we were right beside the Arctic Ocean, nobody was talking about team experiences ... nobody mentioned so much as dipping a toe in.

Chuck suggested we explore the area at once. As the community is spread across a series of islands, the best way to do that is by boat. We knew they hunted beluga whale up here and we were curious to see the hunting grounds, but the seas around Tuk can be treacherous and Chuck didn't seem convinced that we would be able to make it out that far in this wind. While we were chatting, I asked him about the origin of the name Tuktoyaktuk. He told me it means 'caribou', and that the area had always been known as Tuk to the Inuit, after a legend in which a woman saw a group of caribou wade into the water and turn to stone. They say that even today, at low tide you can see reefs that look like these petrified animals.

As we made our way down to the boat, Chuck sniffed the wind and screwed up his face. Then he told us he thought we could try to find the beluga if we took it carefully. I was excited. I'm not keen on whale hunting in principle, but this was a fishing community, and the whales fed the local people through the winter.

I've mentioned how the temperature had dropped, but it wasn't freezing or anything – this was summer, after all. Chuck, however, was wearing gloves and a jacket zipped to the neck with a hood over his head. I assumed it was going to be really chilly on the open water, and I said as much to him.

'No,' he said. 'This isn't for the cold, Charley. It's for the mosquitoes.'

The boat was tied up to a wooden pontoon, and with the four of us aboard now, Chuck fired up the engine and backed into the bay. Sitting there in the bows, I had to pinch myself. This was the Arctic Ocean, the northernmost point on our expedition and our third frontier.

As he turned the boat, Chuck took a call and told whoever he was speaking to that it was blowing twenty-four knots from the east and would hit thirty tomorrow, so he doubted we'd be able to make the return trip to Inuvik by boat after all. My heart sank a little as I heard him suggest we would have to take a flight back instead. I'd been looking forward to the boat trip; crossing the sea and heading south on the river would've been a great way to travel. But he told us that if the wind was hitting thirty knots, it would be too choppy to make that journey safely.

With the windshield closed and the canopy up to shelter us, we made good headway. We passed a drilling platform, set on a massive, hexagonal exploration vessel. The drilling had not been that successful, and Chuck told us that the oil company had used that bit of kit for only a couple of years.

Now it was just rusting slowly, like some futuristic fort rising from the water to dominate the bay. He took us in close, explaining the local children used the vessel as a playground.

A playground? That sounded right up my street. The water was a little choppy but if the local youngsters could do it, then so could I. With me perched on the bows, Chuck brought the boat in close. I spotted an iron ladder, which led up the side of the vessel to a gap like a square porthole right at the top. Jumping from the pitching boat to the bottom rung, I began to climb as Chuck backed away. I felt like a pirate; a modern-day Jack Sparrow storming another ship.

It was pretty eerie up there. Inside, it was hollow, and the central section where I suppose the rig would have been situated was filled with water. It was weird: Chuck had said the vessel was abandoned twenty years ago, and I would have thought that after that long it would be rusting away to nothing. In fact it was all pretty much as it would have been when the oil company left.

Russ climbed up, too. The longer we were there, the more it felt like being on the set of some futuristic movie, like *Waterworld* maybe. All around the deck were these sealed air vents – between us Russ and I worked the lid off a couple but could see nothing but darkness below. The red-painted helicopter deck was spread with a massive rope net to give the runners some traction when the choppers were landing and taking off. It was coming apart in a few places, but considering its age it was nowhere near as rotten as you would have expected. I gazed back across the bay to the clutch of buildings that made up Tuktoyaktuk. It was the only break in an otherwise desolate horizon. Feeling a little spooked, I headed back to the boat.

Back on the ocean waves, we crossed to one of the smaller islands. Chuck pointed out a building where fishermen hung whales to drain the blubber of moisture before preparing the meat for boiling.

As Chuck eased the boat to the shore, we jumped on to a beach of hard shingle and driftwood to meet Douglas, our host for the night. He looked like a bee-keeper, with a full mosquito net over his head. I was beginning to feel anxious about this. Douglas was busy with a length of twine, his waders folded down to his knees. He had plenty of driftwood piled up, and next to it a massive black cauldron, which I assumed must be for boiling down the whale blubber. He introduced us to his fellow fisherman, Sam, who was working on their boat. In the old days, the Inuit would have used canoes, and I tried to imagine paddling out in one of those, dressed in sealskin with a hand-held harpoon.

Douglas was setting his fishing net, spreading it between a length of driftwood he'd driven into the ground and a buoy about fifty yards out from the shore. Hopefully we would have fresh fish tonight. He was as concerned about the weather as Chuck, telling us that it was too windy to hunt beluga today. He said that it was forecast to hit forty knots, ten more than we'd heard Chuck mention. It really didn't feel that windy, although it was puffing my hair around a little bit, and the water seemed pretty flat, but given what the two Inuits were saying, it didn't look good for a boat trip back tomorrow.

Chuck was going to take us back into town for a while, as a fisherman there had brought in a whale. A couple of women were working on the kill on the beach, along with a young child. We went ashore, and I wandered over to say hello and see what I could learn. I'd never seen anything like this before. Although whaling is the staple industry in this part of the world, this particular catch wasn't part of a commercial venture. The fishermen slaughter whales purely to feed their families through the long winter. A fire was burning under a cauldron like the one we'd seen at Douglas's camp, and I could smell the sweet scent of the whale meat boiling.

The family had a table set up that was sheltered from the wind by a sheet of tarpaulin. It was laid with square sections of white-skinned whale meat. The women were preparing enough of the meat to last the winter, boiling off the fat so they could store it. I asked one of them if it tasted nice and she told me she didn't know; she hadn't tried it yet. She was a friend of 'Chucky', as everyone around here seemed to call our guide, and told us she hadn't eaten whale meat in a while because she'd been working down in Inuvik and had only just come back. She was so rusty she'd had to ask her uncle how to prepare it. Chucky said that once the meat was cooked it was stored, and during the cold months they would microwave what they needed. It tasted best just out of the pot, however, particularly when dipped in HP sauce!

I took a quick look inside the smokehouse, which was very dark. Thick strips of whale meat hung from the ceiling. I have to say, they looked pretty unappetising. Outside again, I messed about on the sand with the small boy who'd been helping with the whale.

Back in the boat again, we ventured as far as Chuck was prepared to go in these conditions. It was windier now – clearly the weather that had been forecast was about to catch up with us. I asked Chuck about the telltale signs that whales were in the area. He said that seagulls were a good indicator;

if you saw them close to the water, that usually meant that whales were hunting, because the birds flew in to pick up scraps. With that in mind, the four of us kept our eyes peeled for any sign of seagulls, as Chucky took us scuttling across the bay.

The further out we went, the choppier it became. The hull of the boat was slapping into the waves so hard I was all but losing my teeth. It was no good – the wind was blowing in the wrong direction and the waves were too big. Chuck said that any beluga in the area would have headed for the relative calm of deeper water, and we had to admit defeat. Who wants to see whales anyway … ?! Spending the night in a whale camp would be enough, and we would have plenty of Arctic mosquitoes for company.

They were everywhere: in your eyes, up your nose, and every time I took a breath I got a great gob-full. Russ had managed to find a net from somewhere and he had it under his cap, around his head, with his jacket zipped up tight and his cuffs pulled down. Even in deepest Africa it had been nothing like this. Is there anywhere in Canada where you're not plagued by mosquitoes? If so, we hadn't been there.

Back at Douglas's camp, we pitched the tent and reinforced the canvas with some plastic tarpaulin. It was a ridge tent and big enough for all of us; it reminded me of the kind you see in the army. With the fire crackling away, Douglas and Chuck got a pot of water boiling and threw in a handful of tea bags. I could see the tea brewing in a swirl of mosquitoes. 'Hey, Charley,' Russ said. 'Remember how the bastards invaded our vodka that time back in Russia?'

I nodded. 'Yeah, we drank them. Served them right, didn't it?'

With the tea brewing – and in a way I'd never seen tea brewed before – we all helped to haul in the net that Douglas and Sam had set earlier. It was hard work, but worth it – it was teeming with fish! And we're not talking minnows here – there were fish of all shapes and sizes: flounders, halibut and little bullheads that we would throw back. Separating them from the net, we cleaned and gutted the keepers and tossed the rest back. Now we really did feel like genuine Inuit fishermen. It was the easiest fishing I've done: string the net, let it soak, and a couple of hours later haul back an impressive catch.

Sam had plenty of tin foil to wrap the fillets in to make sure they wouldn't burn when we cooked them over the open fire. When they were done, we ate them with potatoes and bannock, the local bread that's Scottish in ancestry, sitting at the wooden table. Our hosts, including all their family members, were fantastic – they could not have been more welcoming or accommodating.

When we turned in at around eleven o'clock, crowding into the big tent, it was still as bright as day outside. At this time of year it barely gets dark at all. It was hard to sleep, but it was nice to have a moment to myself to reflect on the day's adventures. The northernmost frontier of Canada was everything I'd hoped it would be. With that thought in my head, I finally fell into a contented sleep.

14

Pickled Toes and Placers

We'd been on the road for well over a month now, and the constant movement and the early mornings were definitely getting to me. We'd joked about mosquitoes, but the incessant biting was wearing us all down. We took the chance to have a couple of days' rest. We've been doing this long enough to know when to take a breather, and it did everyone the power of good. So it was with our batteries recharged that we made our way to the Yukon.

Our next stop was Dawson City, a town famous for being the centre of the Klondike Gold Rush at the end of the nineteenth century. Having started from Canada's easternmost point at Cape Spear, we were now right up in the north-west corner, close to the Alaskan border. The Klondike was the last of what are known as the great gold rushes: first it was California (1848–55), then Victoria in Australia in 1851 and finally up here in 1896–9.

We made our way to the site of Klondike No. 4, the massive land dredger that used to operate here once the main boom was over in the early twentieth century. It was incredibly efficient and very successful, making something like eight million dollars in gold for the company. I can't express how big it is – it's a machine that looks like a building. Covering as much ground as a football pitch, it operated a conveyor belt of iron buckets as tall as I am to scoop out the rock. In 1959, the dam at the head of the valley burst and the flood pushed the dredger against the hillside, where it stayed until the army were sent for to rescue it. Today it sits back in its original position, although the conveyor belt has long since stopped and it's now just a tourist attraction.

I was curious to find out what happened to the gold after it was dug up, and after asking around, I was introduced to a guy called Tyson, who worked for Mid-Arctic Gold Yukon Ltd and had a sign on his door announcing that he was a gold-buyer. He showed me a bowl of gold dust, which was amazing, and explained that individual prospectors are still working 'claims', specific areas where individuals or companies are allowed to prospect. Some of these have been held by the same family for generations and prospectors are still finding gold along the Klondike. They bring it to him and he estimates the quality. That gives him an idea what he should be paying for it, and the company then sells that quantity of their own gold on the market. With the money they make, they pay the miner, then replace what they've sold with the new gold. That way their money always remains in gold.

Tyson is one of only two gold-buyers in Dawson City, and I got the impression there was no love lost between them. They aren't enemies as such, just competitors, and they get all kinds of quantities of gold brought to them – from as little as ten grams of dust to pounds and pounds of the stuff chiselled from hard rock. Tyson had to be careful what he said to us because of course this stuff is valuable and everything he does is confidential. He did tell me, however, that as of 15 July, the price of gold was 1,498 Canadian dollars per ounce, which didn't sound bad.

When he weighed the dust in the bowl and made his calculations, estimating the purity that would remain after melting and refining, it worked out to be just under 17,000 dollars' worth of gold. I was gobsmacked – $17,000 for that little pile! I asked him where I could go to stake a claim.

'Sorry, Charley,' he said. 'They're all taken.'

Tyson was from Vancouver originally, though he

attended the Yukon College in Whitehorse. He came to Dawson City seven years ago, just for a visit, and one night in a bar ran into the guy who would become his boss. He was offered a job that same night and has been a gold-buyer ever since.

The gold dust was pretty grubby-looking, with no glint or lustre to it. That's how it is immediately after it's been separated from the dirt; it's only later, when it's cleaned up and polished, that it begins to look like gold as we understand it. Tyson explained that even after it's been melted, the gold is still roughly the same purity as it was when it came out of the ground. It's only at the refining stage that every impurity is extracted and it ends up as 24 carat, which is as close to 100 per cent pure gold as you can get.

It sounded like quite the process: extracted from the hillside, then brought here to be melted before being shipped to the refinery and on to whatever form it would eventually take – an ingot, or jewellery perhaps. Out the back of Tyson's office was a workshop where they melted the gold in a furnace. It was incredibly hot in there, with the furnace roaring away in one corner, but I was really excited to see how the gold was melted. Tyson poured the dust into a flat, coffin-shaped tray and then mixed it with borax and soda ash, which helped to create what he called a flux, to help shift the impurities and assist the melting process. After that he put on a heavy-duty fire-resistant jacket, welding mask and a pair of massive fireproof mittens. Right at the heart of the red-hot furnace was a smelting cup that he lifted out with a pair of tongs. I had to stand back at this point; the heat was almost unbearable. The tray of dust had a flattened edge that fitted over the cup so that Tyson could pour the mixture in. Using the tongs again, he replaced the cup in the furnace and secured the lid. Twenty minutes later it would be ready to pour.

We'd been told there was still plenty of gold to be had in the Klondike and it could be found pretty much anywhere. So while we were waiting for the dust to melt, I went outside and dug up a shovelful of dirt, which I tipped into a pan and washed in the trough outside. I felt like Charlton Heston in *The Call of the Wild*. Rinsing away the silt and dirt, I saw a tiny speck of yellow among the stones. Gold! A nugget the size of a pinhead, but it was real gold, and all I'd done was take one shovel of dirt from the yard. I could see how easy it would be to catch 'gold fever', and why even today would-be prospectors still came up here in search of their fortune. I was delighted, holding up my tiny nugget for all to see. And then I dropped it. I dropped the bloody thing straight into the gravel at my feet. I could not believe it. I scrabbled around on my hands and knees trying to find it. My gold, my gold . . . where's my bloody gold?

Still bemoaning my loss, I went back to the shed to see how the melt was getting along. The furnace was like a knee-high dustbin with a Polo-mint-shaped hole in the top and a vent in the side where blue flames were spitting out. You really did not want to stand too close to it, believe me. Poking an iron stave through the hole, Tyson gave the mixture a bit of a stir, then took a mould and poured a little oil into it to stop the solidified gold bar from sticking. After that, he grabbed the tongs and lifted the smelting cup out of the furnace. This was the tricky bit. I watched in wonderment as he poured molten gold, licked by flames, into the ingot mould, without spilling a drop.

Of course he had done this hundreds of times, but I couldn't get my head around the fact that I was watching a guy melt 17,000 dollars' worth of gold. He admitted that the first time he poured gold like that he'd been incredibly nervous – essentially he was pouring molten money, and spilling any would have been a disaster. Thankfully he never has. If it was me, I know my hands would be too wobbly – I'd be bound to drop the thing and spill some prospector's fortune all over the floor.

A little while later he handed me a solid gold bar about the size and shape of a small bar of chocolate. When we weighed it, Tyson reckoned that it was around 83 per cent pure, which increased the value by $500.

I could see how the business was built on trust; with no regulatory body overseeing things, it was a gentleman's agreement between the miner, the gold-buyer and the assayer: a price, a handshake and a deal. I liked that; it smacked of how it was in the old days. Tyson said that the method of exchange hadn't really changed at all for over a century.

We all had gold fever now, so Tyson made a few calls, trying to hook us up with a prospector named Dave who worked a number of claims along the river valley. It turned out Dave had been in the hospital down south because of a water-skiing accident and wouldn't be able to meet us until later, but his brother Dirk was waiting for us at the main claim, sitting on a massive broken-down Caterpillar excavator. He told us that this claim had been in the family since 1974 and occupied a strip of land in Gold Bottom Creek, which was the spot where Robert Henderson, a Nova Scotian who had come north from Colorado, discovered the first gold on the Klondike in 1896. Dave worked the claim on his own now, though Dirk had worked with him in the past. This was actually his first day back in eighteen years, and he'd only agreed to come up because of Dave's accident and the duff Caterpillar.

At this point Dave showed up, so we went to meet him and left Dirk to fix the excavator's fan belts. Dave had a big smile and a dry sense of humour. He explained that the area he worked was a 'placer mine', which meant they were bringing up gold that was lying loose in the gravel rather than being part of the rock. He told me that there are three basic processes in placer mining: first you remove what he called the overburden (that's the permafrost); once that's done, you can get on with the sluicing process; and finally you go into what he referred to as the clean-up. The gold is found in the bedrock, beneath the overlying mud. Dave works with the bulldozer or excavator to remove the top layers, but when he hits gravel he starts to pan by hand, just like in the old days. Once he sees gold, he stops panning and starts sluicing the gravel instead.

His father was the one who started mining this area, beginning with six claims. Dave has expanded that to more than seventy now. He's had to expand because when his father had it the ground was 'virgin', but now they're much further off the 'pay streak', as they say. It's a lot more difficult to find gold these days, but the high price helps.

We'd seen lots of miners in Dawson already, and Dave confirmed that there was another gold rush going on – plenty of people arriving with the fever. But it wasn't for placer mining – they were here to mine hard rock. I was amazed to hear that even after a hundred years of mining up here they were still looking for the mother lode. Hard-rock mining is a much heavier business – operators need lots of chemicals and crushing machines – whereas placer mining is fundamentally the washing of dirt. Dave told us that for almost forty years now his family have been taking dirt out of the ground, washing it and putting it back.

It's an expensive business – Dave was constantly fixing or updating machinery, and he told me that every ounce of gold he took from the ground was sold to keep the business operating. I'd heard that some miners kept gold back and watched how the prices were going, but Dave didn't buy into that. His view was that unless you had another source of income, every bit you found went straight to buyers like Tyson in order to keep operating. He showed me how he screened the gold after sluicing the gravel and then panning. There were three different sieves, one on top of the other so the gold would filter through. After this we came to what he described as the only fun part of the whole operation.

He was talking about the Gold Wheel – a strange-looking contraption with an inverted circular pan that spins at an angle on a wheel with water pouring over it. They're commercially available now, but the one Dave was using had actually been built by his father. The wheel is the final process; it separates the gold from the last residue of dirt, dust and stones. Dave poured a cup of gold on to the wheel, and the water washing over it removed the final bits of debris. What was left was just like what I had seen earlier in Tyson's office.

During the gold rush of 1896–9, five thousand people had occupied this valley. A whole town had sprung up, and yet today only one family and one wooden building remain. Inside that building the walls are decked with old photos showing how the area looked at the turn of the twentieth century: shops, hotels, a post office, even a hospital. Having seen how a placer mine worked, and learned something about the history of the area, there was one more thing we had to do in Dawson City: hit up the Dawson Hotel for a sour-toe cocktail.

Yes, you read that right: sour-toe cocktail. The story goes back to just before the Second World War, when a prospector named Captain Dick bought a cabin in the hills not far from here. The fellow he bought it from had built it and lived there with his brother. When the brother passed away, all that remained of him was a big toe he'd lost to frostbite some years before, and which had been pickled in alcohol. When Captain Dick bought the cabin, it came complete with the pickled toe. After showing it off in various bars, he came up with the idea of dropping it into his cocktail and kissing the toe as he drank. Captain Dick is long gone, of course, but the tradition has continued, and if you go to the Dawson Hotel, you'll find the current custodian of the toe, Ed. As we ordered our drinks, he unpacked an ugly brown curly thing from a piece of tissue paper. At first glance it could have been a small turd, but actually it was a shrivelled human toe. Ed told me the original toe got swallowed by mistake a long time ago, and I asked him where the replacement had come from. 'There've been a few, actually,' he told me. 'People donate them, though we only take one at a time,' he added. 'If you ever have a toe amputated, we'd love to have it.' With that, he dunked the toe in my drink and I kissed it as tradition demanded.

The following morning we were up early to jump on a plane from Dawson to Silver City. The plane was a Beaver, built in 1958, with a single rotary engine. I could see all the pistons gathered around the cylindrical head beyond the propeller. It was that kind of principle that gave birth to the BMW Boxer motorbike engine, and the Boxer is a cracking bike. We were flying south from a tiny airstrip carved out of the hills. The pilot, Matt, ran a little company called Tintina Air and had twelve years' experience of flying in this area, which was good to know, as there were a lot of tall mountains to negotiate. The Yukon's highest peak is Mount Logan, which at just under 20,000 feet is second only to Alaska's Mount McKinley in the whole of North America. I joined Matt upfront for the flight, which would take an hour and forty-five minutes. The plan was to make our way out on to the glacier, where, if the weather held, I'd be taught the rescue training I mentioned earlier.

As we gained altitude, the view out of the window was spectacular: the green valley around Dawson, the Klondike River and the mine tracings that looked like massive caterpillars peeling off it. From above you could see that for all the gold that had been found, the mining really had ruined this valley. Matt and I talked about the current boom and how it had brought so many people up here – having been born in the Yukon, he was more than happy about that. His company had just bought another plane, and he told me it was nice to be able to make a decent living.

This was a single-stick plane, but the controls could swivel between the pilot's seat and the passenger's. I'd had a few flying lessons, so pretty early on in the journey, Matt shifted the stick across. It was amazing to be flying such an old plane through this beautiful scenery, but at 120 miles an hour, we were touching down in Silver City in no time. There we were met by a young woman named Sian, who was going to take us on to the glacial slopes of Mount Logan. Another mountain. God, I hoped it wasn't going to be like the last one. Sian assured me it wouldn't be anything like that terrifying ridge I still saw in my dreams. Or rather, nightmares.

When we'd driven out on to the Athabasca Glacier a few days earlier, our guide Jason had said that he didn't think anyone could rescue themselves from a glacier if they happened to take a tumble down a crevasse. I had visions of Joe Simpson in *Touching the Void*, but Sian did her best to persuade me that it would be nothing like that; this was a safety drill, nothing more, and nothing a guy like me could not handle. A guy like me! She had no idea who she was dealing with ... One look at Russ's face and you could see he was thinking the same thing. Anyway, onward and, hopefully, upward. They had already sent some gear up to the glacier by plane, and Sian was waiting for the pilot to come back with a full weather report, because although the skies seemed clear enough today, it had been storming quite badly and we were due to camp up there. If a storm decided it liked the area and settled, it could keep us trapped for days.

Sian was right: this was nothing like Mount Fable. That had been Alberta in the heat; this was the Yukon in the ice and snow. Kitted out with boots and waterproof gaiters, I followed Sian up the slope. Russ had gone on ahead and was waiting outside a pair of massive tunnel-shaped tents, like those you see at permanent bases in Antarctica. Inside they had everything, including beer, which is always a good sign – and we had no worries about keeping it cold up here.

The tent was fitted with a stove and a long table, everything we would need if we did happen to get snowed in for a week or so. The pilot had reported a fog bank that was headed this way, and though the sun was shining outside and we were only wearing T-shirts, Sian reckoned that in less than two hours we would not be able to see our hands in front of our faces. That meant we ought to crack on with the training.

She fitted me out with snow shoes for the one-kilometre walk up the mountain to the crevasse, which I was pleased to hear was wide and shallow, not deep and dark. Mercifully, there were no mosquitoes and I was able to walk unmolested. We were on the Discovery Ice Field, a small part of the St Elias Ice Fields, which comes third only to the North and South Pole in terms of its vast size. Thinking about that, I decided that if I was going to fall down a glacier, at least it was a serious one and I could brag about it.

We climbed higher and higher; the pack ice was firm enough underfoot, but Sian told me that out near the ocean, the glacier is wasting away pretty quickly. I was surprised, and somewhat alarmed, to hear that the melt from St Elias could potentially be responsible for a two-centimetre rise in the level of the oceans right across the world, which could be interesting for a place like London . . .

We were closing in on the glacier now, the slope getting steeper and the crags ahead covered in ice and snow. As we roped up, Russ was looking at the sky and wondering aloud about the fog. I was just thinking about the drop I'd be rappelling into. Once Sian had the rope fixed, we were off again, with her leading the way on her snow shoes. I padded after her, my nerves tingling.

Finally we arrived. The crevasse was a great cleft in the snow, a drop of about thirty feet. Even in the daytime, I didn't see it until we were right on it, and I could appreciate how easy it would be to fall in. While we fixed a belay, Sian and I chatted about climbing, and I told her about my ascent of Mount Fable with Barry Blanchard. She used to date a climber who hung out with Barry, until her dad told her that she could date anyone she wanted as long as he was not a climber or a pilot, because in this part of the world they tended to die young.

Sian would be showing us a technique she referred to as a 'self-evacuation', which is what a climber should do if they fall into a crevasse on the end of a rope. I'd have to 'prusik' my way out, which is how you get up the rope if there are no foot- or handholds available. I watched her prepare the gear and demonstrate the knots for the prusik loops I'd soon have to tie myself. They are very specific – they have to be just right in order for the loop to slide up the rope – and Sian wasn't going to tie them for me. I would have to do that myself when I hit the bottom.

Of course the longer it took to get ready, the more hairy the whole situation became. It's always the waiting that gets you. It had been like that at the river rapids, looking down on that washing machine of a vortex, and it was the same up here. By the time everything was set, the butterflies were fluttering away like there was no tomorrow.

Sian demonstrated what I would have to do, dropping nonchalantly over the edge of the crevasse. She then climbed up again swiftly, using the rope and making it look easy. When she fastened me to the rope, I fell strangely silent. I was concentrating on remembering the knots; I couldn't take the embarrassment of being hauled back up by someone else. It was now or never. 'Fuck it,' I said to anyone listening. 'Let's do it.' And with that, I backed up to the edge.

Sian told me just to lean back and walk down, easing the rope through the descender one-handed. It was a long way down – no pun intended. Hesitating to begin with, I slipped a little, but then I got comfortable with the rope and bobbed my way down to the dark chasm at the bottom of the crevasse. Climbing up again was much harder than abseiling down. It was back-breaking work and you really would not choose to do it unless there was no other way. It took ages; every time I managed a few inches I thought I would slip back, and the toll it took on my arms was incredible.

I made it to the top, though, sweating hard and rolling on my back in the snow as I emerged into the daylight. To celebrate we had a bit of a toboggan race, sliding down the hill back to camp. I was really delighted to have accomplished something else so challenging – crossing another personal frontier – and to be up that high with the sky so still and the sun blazing down on freshly fallen snow.

15

Trains, Planes and Motorbikes

Back in Silver City after a chilly night's camping, we headed for Jasper, where we'd be catching a train. I was exhausted; we'd had a lot of fun, but that climb had taken its toll. We'd had our fair share of early mornings on this trip, and had combined them with quite a few late nights, which is never a good idea. But the next stage ought to be relaxing – riding a massive train called the Rocky Mountaineer, which would take us through the mountains to a place called Kamloops. From there we would be back on the bikes as far as Lillooet.

The railway is very important in Canada – it is used to

carry a lot of freight, and it's not uncommon to see trains over a kilometre in length, with as many as half a dozen diesel locomotives pulling them. What makes the Mountaineer so special is that it has these fantastic panoramic domed roofs so that you can really enjoy the scenery. I was excited by the thought of sitting back and watching some of the most beautiful landscapes in the world go by. With the end of the expedition now in sight, this was one train ride I was really going to relish.

There was no raised platform at the station, just a long strip of pavement at ground level, which gave us a strong impression of just how big this train was. Russ (a massive train fan, remember?) had arranged this part of the journey. He'd made the right calls and spoken to the right people, and we were booked into the last car, which had a viewing platform with an uninterrupted vista behind. There was no better place to view the passing landscape.

Inside, the train's manager, Peter, greeted us and told us that he'd be looking after us during our journey. This was getting good. We'd been roughing it for nigh on two months now – this tent and that piece of hard ground, complete with its million and one mosquitoes – so a little bit of comfort would not go amiss. Peter told us he would do all he could to make our journey enjoyable; the only thing he couldn't control was the drizzling rain.

He led us into the dining car, where shortly they would be serving breakfast. In the galley-style kitchen, a number of chefs were preparing the food. The smells were just amazing; I was beginning to salivate now. The head chef told me there were four kitchens on the train to cater for the 250 passengers. He was very proud of the food his kitchens produced, explaining that being on the Mountaineer was a real experience and it was important that the right atmosphere was created. As far as he was concerned, they were trying to replicate the kind of experience high-end passengers in the nineteenth century would have enjoyed.

'Do you like to cook?' Chef asked me.

'I love to cook.'

'OK, well maybe we'll let you make a bit of lunch with us later.'

The train was very popular: coach-loads of tourists were gathered on the platform, and it took a while to get everybody on board. I hung out at the back of the train watching the freight cars go by, before finally we were rolling.

I sat down for a chat with some Australians who were criss-crossing Canada by train. We talked about Australia and my various experiences there over the years as we sipped the peach wine that the stewards brought us. The carriage was fantastic: there was so much glass all around us that everything outside the train was plainly visible.

The scenery was truly spectacular. As the train cut through gorges and forests, miles and miles of track spooled out behind us. Some of the individual sections of track come in 850-foot lengths, which makes them easier to lay around corners; there's enough flex in a piece of iron that long to give a little without too much stress. I've been on trains all over the world, but for the luxury and the scenery, nothing could top this.

After breakfast, it was my turn in the kitchen. They fitted me out in a chef's coat and gave me a sockeye salmon to prepare. Chef showed me how to clean it properly – cutting off the head, working from both sides to keep it neat; then removing the bones by slicing along the inside and bringing the skeleton out in one piece. After that I filleted the fish, removing the flesh from the skin and cutting it into lengths. As we cooked up some fresh green beans, we discussed the way that fine cooking has become such a part of mainstream society. With all the TV chefs and cookery programmes, it is no longer an elitist thing, and the variety of tastes and ingredients from all over the world has added a whole new dimension to the chef's role.

I've always fancied myself as a bit of a cook, actually. (My dad reckons I have this knack of being able to knock up some gravy or a sauce out of just about anything.) Together Chef and I made a side dish of fried potatoes with roasted peppers, then added a sprinkling of beans and the salmon fillet on top. The final flourish was a mustard-seed vinaigrette. I have to say it looked beautiful when Chef did it . . . and not *too* bad when I had a go.

Sitting in the dining car eating a fillet of sockeye that I had helped to prepare, I was in heaven.

'So, Russ,' I said, between mouthfuls. 'This bit of the expedition isn't quite so extreme really, is it?'

He was silent.

'But it is *extremely* nice,' I added, spearing another piece of delicious salmon with my fork.

By the time we rolled into Kamloops, I felt really refreshed and was itching to get back on my bike. Throwing on my jacket and helmet, I set off, beetling along through the heart of one of the most majestic mountain ranges anywhere on earth. It was poetry. With the road unravelling in delicious twists and turns, I was really enjoying this opportunity to mess about on the bike. It was only when we pulled over for a breather that I started to wonder what it would be like to view this amazing landscape from above.

I mentioned to Russ what I was thinking, and in the next town we stopped at a petrol station to ask whether anyone knew of anywhere we could hitch a ride in a glider. As luck would have it, about fifty miles further down the road there was an airfield with a gliding school run by a Czech guy called Rudy. The owners of the petrol station gave us a phone book and we found the number and spoke to Rudy. He told us that the weather wasn't brilliant, but if we got a wriggle on we could have some time in the air before the next storm blew in.

We jumped back on the bikes and increased our speed, keen to get to Rudy's before the weather turned. It wasn't long before we found the signs for the turn-off and rode down to a grassy airstrip, where we spotted a couple of the engineless aeroplanes. Rudy was waiting for us.

'OK, Charley,' he told me, after the introductions were over. 'You can sit in the front. I'll be in the back seat, doing the flying from there. But there is a control stick in the front, so you can help if you want.'

Prodding the aluminium fuselage, I told him I thought it looked a little thin.

'Yeah,' he said. 'It's made out of beer cans ... we just straighten them out and build it. Simple really.' I hoped he was joking.

Rudy told me that gliding was about being at one with

nature; when the aircraft rides the thermals, it's not uncommon to have an eagle riding them right alongside you. I was really excited now – that was exactly what I'd hoped to hear. I hauled one leg after the other into the glider, which was so low to the ground it felt like getting into the cockpit of a go-kart. Rudy handed me the obligatory sick bag, just in case, and I stuffed it down beside me. 'I don't want any early exiting,' I shouted back to him. 'I don't want to turn around and find you've bailed out!'

'Don't worry,' he said. 'I'll be with you every loop-the-loop of the way.'

The tow plane started to pull us along the runway – it really was pretty smooth – and in barely a moment we were up in the air. As we climbed, I asked Rudy how he came to be living in Canada. He explained how he'd grown up under the communist regime in Czechoslovakia, and although he'd hated it, he'd taken advantage of support from various agencies and learned to fly gliders for free. When he was twenty-six, he'd bought himself a holiday in Cuba, one of the few places Czechs were allowed to travel to. At Montreal, where the plane was due to refuel, he got off with the other passengers but didn't get back on again. Claiming asylum, he was eventually allowed to stay. One day he was hiking in these mountains, took in the view and thought how cool it would be to glide up here, so he and a friend raised the money to buy a glider and tow plane, and the rest, as they say, is history.

We were up in the air with the grey and green mountains surrounding us. All I had to do was sit there and take in the view. I was so pleased we'd had this spontaneous idea, and that Canada was the kind of place where there was a gliding school round every corner! From up there I could see a whole mass of dirt roads; the mountains had originally been opened up by loggers. Rudy said that if they carried enough fuel, dirt-bike riders could go for days and days without bumping into anybody. He explained that beyond the logging roads were animal trails, and you could ride from place to place on those without ever even touching a road. That sounded amazing, and I made a mental note to come back here one day and do just that. Wow, I could see a whole new TV series shaping up . . .

We were out over the river now, and it was just beautiful. Beyond that we flew over a First Nations village, where Rudy pointed out their road system, which was laid out in the shape of an eagle's head.

It was pretty misty up there. The clouds were low and swirling around the snow-capped peaks, which seemed to be gathered closely around us. Rudy said that gliding was challenging with the mountains so close, and you really did have to concentrate. We'd been attached to the tow plane until now, but suddenly it peeled off, right between a couple of steep peaks, and now Rudy really came into his own, veering off to the left, circling, trying to catch a thermal and find a little bit of lift. It was silent now – nothing but the wind rattling the canopy.

As we drifted lower, I spotted a waterfall. From this vantage point, the way it tumbled down the wall of rocks was incredibly dramatic. As he had promised, Rudy threw a loop, and suddenly I was upside down. Instinctively I grabbed hold of my harness, keeping my breathing regular, and for a split second I felt almost weightless. It was an incredible feeling, something I've never experienced before.

We were in really rugged terrain now, with nothing that even vaguely resembled civilisation nearby. Rudy told me that this was what pilots called 'lion country', and you really did not want to land unless you had no choice. He meant mountain lions, of course, pumas or cougars, which can reach a couple of hundred pounds in weight and roam from Alaska all the way into South America. They've been known to take hikers and mountain bikers when they're particularly hungry.

I kept my breathing even and steady as Rudy threw another loop. It was warm in the glider, and by this point I was a little bit sweaty and feeling just a tad nauseous, too. But it was my turn to take the controls, and any thoughts of sickness left me pretty quickly as I concentrated on flying. It wasn't easy – the steering was very subtle – but having flown a few planes in my time, I did all right. Of course, with me at the helm we found the lift we'd been wanting and began to gain altitude.

Back on the ground, I lay on my belly in the grass and reflected on it all. I still felt a little sick, and I was reminded of how I'd felt when I climbed out of that Spitfire in Australia on *Right to the Edge*. God, that was awful. I'm lucky, though – very few people get to do this stuff, *and* get paid while they're doing it. Believe me, having spent years working as a painter and decorator, I know how fortunate I am.

There was no rest, though; it was back on the bikes as we headed down to Whistler for another kind of bike ride altogether. Rudy had talked about dirt-bike riders on the trails up here, but he'd also told me that plenty of people use the same trails for mountain biking and horse riding. As we hadn't been on a pedal bike of any kind thus far, I reckoned we'd have to rectify that before the expedition was over.

This wasn't just any old bike ride, however; this was extreme: a helicopter flight to the start of the route on one of the mountains, followed by a dash down to the base.

Whistler is renowned for mountain biking, and this was intense stuff we were undertaking. I'd just been flying above those mountains; I'd ridden my motorbike through them and I'd climbed up them, so now I had to finish off in true Whistler style.

We took one chopper while the bikes followed on another, strapped together and dangling underneath so they could be dropped to where we were on the mountain. I wasn't going to be riding alone; Mungo was filming, and I had my guide, Mark, with me to protect me from mountain lions and make sure I didn't break any bones at the hands of some monstrous tree root or rock. It was seriously rugged up here.

As I was gazing out the window of the chopper, I heard Mark say something about riding on a ridge. After my experiences climbing in Calgary, I wasn't good with ridges, and I could feel the nerves beginning to kick in. But we had another guide, Dave, riding with us, so there were two experts as well as the two novices, which ought to help if things went wrong on the way down.

We set off riding over the snow, but I took a tumble right away – the front wheel washed out and I ended up sprawled in the white stuff. I was OK – the only thing hurt was my pride – but after that inauspicious start we walked the bikes across the next section. Mark and Dave wouldn't let us get away with that for long, though, and we were soon pedalling again, heading for the rocks and trees at what felt like breakneck speed. Even with all that space, an entire mountain, a couple of us still managed to collide. My heart was pumping like crazy and the adrenalin seemed to be flowing out of control.

We'd done a lot of extreme things since we left Cape Spear, but this was one of the gnarliest. The entire way down all you could hear was the howl of brakes and people swearing. It was as intense as anything I've ever done, way more difficult than being on a motorbike. It was also energy-sapping in a way I hadn't been prepared for at all.

After a while the snow disappeared and we were riding over dirt, scrub and rock. Mark suggested we take an old mining trail known as Viper, which according to him was pretty 'out there'. We had arrived in Whistler at the same time as the Crankworx mountain-biking festival, which meant that the main bike routes would be busy, so the trail sounded like a good idea. Dave, however, sounded a note of caution.

'Charley,' he said. 'Just so you know. If we take this old prospector's trail, we're on our own. If anything goes wrong, we have to make it out of there by ourselves. OK?'

'OK,' I said, with a quick glance at Mungo. 'Let's do it then, shall we? Let's go.'

We dropped off the main route on to the trail, and I could

see at once that Dave had not been kidding; this was the boonies for sure. We were on a tiny path between the trees, with really steep drops that had me clamping on the brakes with both hands so hard I was all but over the handlebars. At one point it was almost sheer – the trail just plummeted to the floor fifteen feet below. As I sat and looked at it, a kid came racing by and took the drop as if it was just another turn before carrying on his way. Dave and Mark made the jump too, both hitting the deck below without so much as a murmur, then they were into a left-hander where the back wheel was off the ground again. Nope, there was no way I was doing that. There was an easier way through the trees, and at this point in the expedition I was really looking forward to seeing my family. I wasn't about to risk my neck now. I wasn't the only one; the muddy trail alongside the path was littered with footprints where other people had pulled up and padded back after making a similar decision. I can hear my dad now, talking about the path of least resistance, and floating downriver rather than swimming against the tide. I'm sorry, Dad, but you really had to be there . . . The fact is, I managed most of the descent from the top of the mountain, but I couldn't bring myself to make that drop, no matter how extreme the buzz might have been.

'Charley!' Dave yelled. 'You wuss! I thought you did the Dakar?'

'That was different,' I informed him. 'I had an engine. And anyway, I broke both thumbs along the way.'

I did manage a couple of smaller jumps here and there, landing hard enough on the saddle to give my single testicle a bit of grief, but it was all in the name of honour. Little by little we careened our way to the valley floor below. It was mind-blowing fun but really tough, and I was absolutely knackered when finally we made it back to Whistler.

16
Underground Overground

We spent the night in Whistler, sharing war stories about mountain-biking exploits. Dave and Mark were competing in the Crankworx mountain-biking festival, alongside people who'd travelled from all over the world. Mark said it was the busiest week in Whistler's calendar by far. The next morning we were up and about very early having a wander through the town, then a quick breakfast and back on the bikes for the glorious ride to the ferry at Horseshoe Bay. From there we would cross to Vancouver Island, the final frontier on this amazing expedition.

We'd spent a lot of time on the trip at high altitude: climbing, gliding, riding. But apart from a brief foray into the mine at Drumheller, we'd not really explored this great country's nether regions. So for our last challenge, we'd be going subterranean. We had been told a while back about the Horne Lake Caves on Vancouver Island, and had come to a team decision that we would make them our last physical frontier before we rode into Tofino. Our guide was Shane, a caver from Australia, who told us that he had come here for a holiday and never really left. He had a climbing background, which makes sense, because if you think about it, the two activities share great similarities. Much of the gear is the same; you're just going down first instead of up.

The path led us right through the forest, which was eerily silent. There was nothing in the trees, no birds singing, no animals moving – in fact the only thing I could hear was Russ, Nat and Mungo jabbering away. I was keen to find out more about the caves from Shane. He told me that nobody really knew anything about their history until the point when they were logged on a geological report in 1912. Only two caves were discovered initially – what they called the Main and the Lower Main – and for years afterwards they were only really known about by the logging crews who cut timber in the area. Then in 1941 the Riverbend Cave was discovered, and in 1963 the Euclataws Cave. The whole region was granted park status in 1971.

It was an uphill climb to get to where we could access the caves, and halfway there a second guide, Richard, joined us.

He told me that some of the earliest cave systems to be explored were in Britain and France, and that most of the gear they used here had been developed in France. He explained that all the caves in the Horne Lake system are connected, though you can't get through them all because in some places the connection is a gravel bed and the only way to tell they're linked is from the water system that seeps through.

We crossed a dry creek bed that for half the year is a raging torrent. It was that creek that led to the discovery that the caves are connected. Richard told me that the water found a crack in the mountain, and made its way hundreds of metres down before coming out again and forming another creek further down the valley. He explained that the forest was what they call second growth – the original trees, which had been logged seventy years before but whose stumps were still visible, would have been much bigger and thicker. What we could see now was natural regrowth, since back then logged areas were not replanted. It was a good example of nature's resilience: a whole new forest in less than a hundred years. It was a totally different story underground, however. Both Richard and Shane were keen to point out that any damage in the caves took so long to repair that all visits were designed to have zero impact on the sediments and crystal formations.

The entrance to the cave was a hole in the ground that had been boarded over with a door cut in the middle. You had to sit down and shuffle your legs through first, then slide your body around so you could climb down the fixed iron ladder. From there we picked our way down through a series of big boulders. I tried to imagine what it would have been like to be the first person down here. The lamps on our helmets were the only lights we had, and the beams bounced across the rock, picking out the crystal formations Richard had been talking about.

He pointed out where we could and couldn't walk; what we could and couldn't touch – in particular the brain rock that grew up in places underfoot. That's exactly what it looked like: pale limestone with bulbous growths of calcite that resembled the lobes of the brain. It was forty thousand years old, and if we damaged it, it would take another forty thousand years before anyone coming after us could see what we were seeing now.

To our right, a great bank of calcite reached deep into a recess. It grows at the rate of a millimetre a century, which meant it was millions of years old. We continued on down – some of the rock was moist and slippery, and we had to be careful where we placed our hands. In places the roof was very low and we were forced to crawl, sliding across a bed of stones or slick limestone on our stomachs, using elbows and knees to worm our way to the next cave. It was really hard work and very claustrophobic, especially when we moved from a crawl-way that measured one body length to one that was more than five. The roof of rock pressing down on my back put me in mind of the coal mine, and Jay's talk about 'squeeze'.

When we were through that long crawl-way, we took a much-needed breather. It was not just the exertion that was tiring, but the way the mountain seemed to weigh down upon you. Richard told us that originally the crawl-way had been full of water; for years anyone who came down here thought it was the end of the cave, so nobody bothered to explore any further. Then one day some 'crazy chick' called Stephanie held her breath, slipped into the crawl-way and came up on the other side. From there she discovered three more hours of caves that led right into the heart of the mountain.

'Hang on a minute,' Russ said. 'You're telling us that a woman went through that tunnel underwater, not knowing if there was another side?'

'Yeah.' Richard nodded. 'That's about the size of it.'

'But you can't turn round in there; what if it was a dead end?'

'Then she'd have had to crawl backwards.'

'You can't do that,' Russ said.

'Sure you can.' Richard smiled. 'If your life depends on it.'

He explained that the tunnel wasn't full of water for its entire length. At one point there was an air pocket between the water and the ceiling, and Stephanie was able to suck a lungful before going on. Even so, it was a hell of a thing to do. What an achievement, to be the person who unearthed this whole section of caves by taking an unknown crawl-way underwater.

Before we carried on, Richard pointed out what he called the 'chilli pepper' – a delicate protrusion of calcite that had been there for ever. We had to be really careful as we made our way past it. We were walking again now, water underfoot and keeping our heads low. The cave was covered in tiny stalactites hanging from the ceiling – they're hollow in the middle, with the water actually coming down a sort of tube. Every time a drop falls off, it leaves a residue of particles, and that's how the stalactite grows. It was all amazing stuff. We were not just exploring the bowels of Canada, but learning how they were formed and discovered, and all about the crystals, the calcite deposits that give them such significance.

We were 120 metres into the system already, and 20 metres down. It was mad to think of all that earth on top of us. Richard told us that by the time we got to the end, we would have travelled 384 metres and dropped 68. The next section was more technical, and here we took out the harnesses we had brought with us in drag bags. I was getting pretty good with a harness by now, and could buckle up without any help. I also felt pretty comfortable abseiling after all my adventures on this trip, and I made my way down into an amazing open space. This wasn't a cave; it was a cavern. From the tight squeeze, the claustrophobia of those crawl-ways, it was suddenly majestic. The roof above our heads was covered in calcite, almost like something alive clinging to the stone. The deeper we went, the greater the deposits of calcite became. The colours down there were amazing – not just grey rock, but pale stone, ochre and gold – and the only sounds were the constant trickle of water running down the walls and the occasional echo of our own voices.

Finally we got to the China Cave, where water tumbles the height of a seven-storey building. I was really into this now – after my tentative effort abseiling on the glacier, I was full of confidence and bounced all the way to the floor. One of the guys in our group, Don, had told me earlier that he was more scared of heights than any other person on the planet. Standing at the top of that cave, looking down into nothing but a black hole, he was absolutely terrified. Eventually he managed to trust his rope and began to make his way down. But the fear didn't leave him until he touched the bottom, where I was waiting to help him unclip his harness. He was a massive guy, well over six feet, yet he was trembling like a newborn lamb.

'Charley,' he said, 'I have never been more scared in my life. I don't know how I did that. I think I must've been more worried about what you guys would say, though, the ignominy of having to be hauled back up.'

I knew how he felt. 'Don,' I said, trying to reach up and pat him on the shoulder. 'The thing is, you overcame your fear.'

Shane led us through the next set of tunnels, where the calcite was formed like rows of whale's teeth. Underfoot the water was getting deeper. We were almost there now; after just a few more twists and turns, we came to the end of the road. Our 384 metres had been accomplished, and we were almost 70 metres under the earth. I don't know what we'd been expecting – something a little more dramatic than the way the roof just gradually dipped until it met the tunnel floor in nothing more romantic than a grubby puddle.

'What did you want?' Richard asked. 'Starbucks or something? It's a tunnel, guys; a hole in the ground.'

He was right, of course; what more could we expect? It *was* a hole in the ground. But we'd made it as far as anybody could, pushed the boundary as far as it could be pushed, and all that was left was to climb out again. We took a minute to pause and reflect on all that we'd done. This blocked tunnel was our final extreme frontier. We had been 3,000 metres up Mount Fable, and now we were 384 metres underground. It called for champagne, but not one of us had remembered to bring a bottle. Oh well, I'd make do with a high five from our guide instead.

'OK,' I said. 'The final frontier and no champagne, so the last man out buys the beer.'

17

Bikes to the Bone

We were coming to the end of our trip. Sitting there underground, I reflected on what had been an incredible journey: an expedition where we had gone from east to west, south to north; up a mountain and deep underground. It had been hard at times, but I had loved every minute of it.

We spent the night in Nanaimo, the third oldest city in British Columbia. This area had once been the site of five First Nations villages. These days it's a city of some 80,000 people, with a bustling night life and a really busy harbour. It's also a haven for bikers, something we had been counting on, because it was from Nanaimo that we were setting out on the very last leg of our journey. In true Boorman style, we had let it be known that we were in the area, and had invited local bikers to join us on a ride across Vancouver Island. Our last stop was Tofino on the western coast.

It was really fitting that we were riding the last stretch of our journey with a bunch of enthusiastic Canadian bikers. One of the things that had struck all of us was how well people had taken care of us; the way we had been welcomed and wished well on every step of this epic expedition. I did have to point out that if they crashed on the convoy it was their own fault, though – nothing to do with us – and that got a laugh.

Our convoy gathered in downtown Nanaimo. The route had been organised by Don, the guy who had been with us in the caves. When we'd told him what we had planned, he'd said he'd ride with us, and suggested that we stop about halfway at a place called Coombs Market, where we could grab a cup of coffee. Now he made the point that although we had informed the RCMP what we were doing, we had no escort, so we should ride carefully, particularly at intersections. I added that in my opinion wheelies were completely acceptable. After that, all that was left for me to do was thank Mungo and Nat for filming the adventure, and Russ not only for organising the whole thing with Lisa and the team back home at Big Earth, but for putting up with me again. Standing up on the seat of my bike, I gave the convoy a big thumbs-up. 'Let's ride!' I shouted.

We were off, with Russ and me out front and Mungo and Nat filming the convoy. We had done what we'd set out to do: pushed the boundaries of this marvellous place, explored its many frontiers. We had begun at Cape Spear on a cold June day, with a mist gathered over the sea and dank clouds picking at our clothes. Now here we were a couple of months later on Canada's western tip, with the sun overhead and temperatures warm enough to wear only a T-shirt. Up came my front wheel in celebration. Not only had we really seen what makes Canada such a great country; we'd met a group of new friends, which is what travelling is all about. I'd learned how the country came into being, how parts of it were a haven for American bank robbers and horse thieves, how Sitting Bull took refuge after the Battle of the Little Big Horn. I'd seen coal mines and gold mines; I'd seen how the Inuit hunt beluga and I'd been in a sweat lodge with First Nations people. Together Russ and I had dived on wrecks in fresh-water lakes, climbed mountains and explored underground. I'd ridden in a rodeo and paddled the waters of the great Bloodvein River. I knew we really had got under the skin of the place.

As Don had suggested, we pulled into the parking lot of a café at Coombs Market for a break, about halfway into our ride. Bike after bike after bike flooded in after us: men and women, young and old, from all walks of life – there must have been 300 in total, and I was so grateful to them for taking the time to come out with us. I made sure I had pictures taken with as many people as possible, and then we were off again. This really was the last leg now.

It's funny, you start out with a mammoth expedition in front of you, and when it comes down to those last few minutes, you can't believe it's over. It's a bit like the summer holidays when you were a child. Did you ever feel like that? When school finished, the summer would yawn ahead, then get chipped away and chipped away until you were struck by the thought that this time next week, this time tomorrow, you would be back at school.

I was looking forward to seeing my family. I haven't mentioned them much in this book, but it's not because they weren't on my mind; they always are. We had just been so busy, and there hadn't been as much riding time as there had been on previous expeditions, hours when I could sit back

257

and let my mind wander. Now I knew I would see them again soon, and I was really excited. Family is everything to me. I'm blessed in having the love of my life as my wife and two marvellous daughters who I dote on.

We were on perfect roads, delicious tarmac, with the kind of mountains you only find in Canada all around us. This country has everything: sea, snow, mountains, ice roads and waterways, as well as mile after mile of rolling prairie. As we got closer to Tofino, the road edged up against the most beautiful lake, and beyond the trees lay the Pacific Ocean. I could smell it; we were here. From Cape Spear to Vancouver, we had crossed a continent.

Just a few minutes left now, but enough time for some seat-standing, some side saddle, some Boorman posing on the bike and a second-gear wheelie that I confess I almost got wrong because I drifted a little too close to the gravel. That could've been a disastrous ending to a staggeringly beautiful journey. The words 'don't try this at home' came to mind, and thinking of my daughters, I rode the final thirty-one kilometres with both wheels firmly on the tarmac.

Someone must have told the Mounties we were coming, because just as we got to our destination, our final frontier, an RCMP pickup came winging by with sirens going and lights flashing to lead us through town. That was really cool, and we followed the truck the last few kilometres through the trees and into Tofino.

Suddenly there it was: a bay of islands thick with trees. People were on the street as the policemen went ahead, with us following like some elongated centipede. I was ecstatic, swept up with the euphoria of the moment. With the bikes parked in one massive line, I walked the length of it thanking each and every one of the people who had turned out to ride with us. It was the perfect way to end an expedition; when you've been travelling for so long with just four of you, roughing it, living on top of each other, to have a group the size of this on the last leg is such a fantastic contrast, you cannot get the smile off your face.

Right at the back was Russ, wearing an *Extreme Frontiers* T-shirt with an *Extreme Frontiers* sticker on his bike, sitting there grinning like a Cheshire cat. That moment summed up the expedition. Gripping his hand, I hugged him. 'Well done, mate,' I said. 'You've done a fantastic job.'

We rode the very last lap down to the water, a little pier where floatplanes were moored alongside the fishing boats. There it was, finally, the Pacific Ocean under a blazing sun and the bluest of blue skies.

For a moment, with all the emotion that had caught up with me, I gazed across the sea into the distance, and shed a few tears. Then Russ was alongside me, with Mungo and Nat, who had put away the cameras.

'We did it, boys,' I said softly. 'Here we are, the four of us. We made it.'

'Yes, we did,' Russ echoed, and for a moment we all just stood there in silence. 'Listen, though,' he added, 'about—'

I held up a hand. 'Russ,' I said. 'No more, please. Not yet. Just let me have a rest first, will you?'

Acknowledgements

Black Diamond

BMW

Canadian Tourism Commission

Lisa Downs

Louisa Edwards

Jeff Gulvin

Eagle Rider

Nim Singh

Touratech

Anna Westall

Wolfskin

If you've been inspired by
Charley's Canadian adventures,
why not hitch a ride on the back
of his bike and travel the world
to its very limits . . .

*Ewan McGregor and Charley head out
on their first, bestselling travel adventure together.
The boys find themselves going the*

LONG WAY ROUND
Chasing Shadows Across the World
Ewan McGregor *and* Charley Boorman

From London to New York, Ewan and Charley chased their shadows through Europe, Ukraine, Kazakhstan, Mongolia and Russia, across the Pacific to Alaska, then down through Canada and America. But as the miles slipped beneath the tyres of their big BMWs, their troubles started. Exhaustion, injury and accidents tested their strength. Treacherous roads, unpredictable weather and turbulent politics challenged their stamina. They were chased by paparazzi in Kazakhstan, courted by men with very large guns in Ukraine, hassled by the police, and given bulls' testicles for supper by Mongolian nomads.

And yet despite all these obstacles, they managed to ride more than twenty thousand miles in four months, changing their lives for ever in the process. As they travelled they documented their trip, taking photographs and writing diaries by the campfire. *Long Way Round* is the result of their adventures – a fascinating, frank and highly entertaining travel book about two friends riding round the world together and, against all the odds, realising their dream.

'Touching and memorable . . . one for armchair travellers and bike freaks' *Daily Mail*

The intrepid duo return for another incredible bestselling adventure, and this time it's going to take them a

LONG WAY DOWN
An African Adventure
Ewan McGregor *and* Charley Boorman

After their fantastic trip round the world in 2004, fellow actors and bike fanatics Ewan McGregor and Charley Boorman couldn't shake the travel bug. And after an inspirational UNICEF visit to Africa, they knew they had to go back and experience this extraordinary continent in more depth.

And so they set off on their 15,000-mile journey with two new BMWs loaded up for the trip. Joining up with producer/directors Russ Malkin and David Alexanian and the *Long Way Round* team, their route took them from John O'Groats at the northernmost tip of Scotland to Cape Agulhas on the southernmost tip of South Africa.

Riding through spectacular scenery, often in extreme temperatures, Ewan and Charley faced their hardest challenges yet. With their trademark humour and honesty they tell their story – the drama, the dangers and the sheer exhilaration of riding together again, through a continent filled with magic and wonder.

Branching out on his first solo trip, Charley is now facing the most dangerous and exciting race in the world. It's time to join the

RACE TO DAKAR
Charley Boorman
With a Foreword by Ewan McGregor

In 2004 Charley Boorman completed his astonishing round-the-world bike trip with his friend, Ewan McGregor. The journey left him exhausted, exhilarated and hungry for a new challenge. And what greater challenge than the Dakar rally?

Beginning in Lisbon and ending in the Senegalese capital of Dakar, the rally covers 15,000 kilometres of treacherous terrain, and is widely regarded as the most dangerous race on earth. With his team-mates Simon Pavey and Matt Hall, Charley faced extreme temperatures, rode through shifting sands and stinging winds, and faced breakdowns miles from civilisation. Charley recounts his extraordinary adventures through Portugal, Morocco, Western Sahara, Mauritania, Mali, Guinea and Senegal. He also follows the stories of other riders – an eccentric, dedicated band of professionals and rookies who all dream of one thing: reaching the finishing line. *Race to Dakar* is the thrilling account of a race that has captured the imagination of millions.

'Boorman is well on his way to becoming
the Michael Palin of motorbikes'
The Times

Charley is facing a huge new challenge – travelling across continents on another adventure. But he has to get there

BY ANY MEANS
The Brand-New Adventure from Wicklow to Wollongong
Charley Boorman

Bikes have always been Charley's first love, but he also enjoys a challenge. So when the chance comes to travel across three continents 'by any means', he jumps right in.

Grabbing whatever local transport he can get his hands on, Charley travels from his home town in County Wicklow all the way to Australia – a trip of over 20,000 miles through twenty-five countries.

Testing Charley's skills and stamina to the limit, this new journey offers him a unique opportunity to meet people and learn first hand all about their countries. He drives a lorry through northern Iran, rides a tuk-tuk through the chaotic and colourful city of Varanasi and becomes the first person ever to wakeboard across the Malay/Singapore border. He sets up his own bus service in Turkey, takes a slow boat down the Mekong, and a very fast one through Borneo to deliver vaccines for UNICEF. And of course he jumps on a bike whenever he can, even if there's a monsoon on the way . . .

*Once again, Charley's braving it in the unknown
and this time he's going*

RIGHT TO THE EDGE
Sydney to Tokyo By Any Means
Charley Boorman

Charley Boorman is back in the saddle for a brand-new, adrenalin-
fuelled adventure!

He begins his journey racing north from Sydney up the Gold Coast,
where he hitches a ride in a Spitfire. In Papua New Guinea he takes a
hand-made canoe through tropical rainforest to stay in a remote tribal
village almost untouched by the outside world. He drives a tuk-tuk
made of bamboo in the Philippines, rides with the Mad Dog biker gang
in Manila and eats deep-fried crickets in Taiwan before reaching his
final destination in Tokyo.

From active volcanoes to coffee plantations to hilltop monasteries,
Charley takes an exhilarating ride through some of the most
spectacular countries in the world. Fast paced and fascinating,
Right to the Edge is a gripping read from one of our very best
travel-adventure writers.

CHARLEY BOORMAN

Bestselling author of
LONG WAY DOWN

EXTREME FRONTIERS
RACING ACROSS CANADA
FROM NEWFOUNDLAND TO THE ROCKIES

DVD AVAILABLE NOW